IN

CHARGE

McDougal & Associates
Servants of Christ and Stewards of the
Mysteries of God

IN CHARGE

Living by Original Design

by

Dr. Abiola Idowu

Published by:

McDougal & Associates
18896 Greenwell Springs Road
Greenwell Springs, LA 70739
www,ThePublishedWord.com

McDougal & Associates is dedicated to spreading the Gospel of the Lord Jesus Christ to as many people as possible in the shortest time possible.

ISBN: 978-1-950398-76-8

Printed on demand in the U.S., the U.K., Australia, and the UAE
For Worldwide Distribution

DEDICATION

Dedicated to all the Kingdom citizens who cost God the life of His Son, Jesus Christ. May your journey on Earth be meaningful as you walk in the truth of the Word of God. It's your season for being *In Charge*.

Shalom!

Contents

Introduction 9

1. Divine Lifting, Your Key To Relevance.......... 17
2. Unwrapping Your Heritage of Freedom........ 61
3. Being Fully In Charge...................................101
4. Living Proof...181
5. Living In a World of Wonders......................231

Other Books by Dr. Abiola Idowu.................281
Author Contact Information 284

I also pray that you will understand the incredible greatness of God's power for us who believe him. This is the same mighty power that raised Christ from the dead and seated him in the place of honor at God's right hand in the heavenly realms. Now he is far above any ruler or authority or power or leader or anything else—not only in this world but also in the world to come.

— Ephesians 1:19-21, NLT

INTRODUCTION

When we know the original intention of the Almighty for creating the Universe, it becomes very easy for us to develop confidence and take our rightful place. The simple truth is that the Earth was created to be ruled and dominated by man, not the devil, not the demons, not the angels, not even the Creator Himself. The Scriptures say:

> *The heaven, even the heavens, are the LORD's; but the earth hath he given to the children of men.* Psalm 115:16

We must never forget the original manifesto of the King:

> *And God said, Let us make man in our image, after our likeness: and let them*

9

> *have dominion over the fish of the sea,*
> *and over the fowl of the air, and over the*
> *cattle, and over all the earth, and over*
> *every creeping thing that creepeth upon*
> *the earth.* Genesis 1:26

The Earth was created to be inhabited by God's children, whom He called man and woman, and His intention is and has been for us to be fully in charge of running the entire Universe.

The Fall of man in the garden of Eden did not change the plan of God. It did delay it for a time, but God is committed to His mission of making man ruler of the Earth.

Because of the Fall, we missed much of what man was supposed to do in running his earthly estate, but now there is a new Man, the last Adam, who came to fulfill the counsel of God and showed us how man must live.

> *But one in a certain place testified, say-*
> *ing, What is man, that thou art mindful*
> *of him? or the son of man, that thou*

visitest him? Thou madest him a little lower than the angels; thou crownedst him with glory and honour, and didst set him over the works of thy hands: thou hast put all things in subjection under his feet. For in that he put all in subjection under him, he left nothing that is not put under him. But now we see not yet all things put under him. But we see Jesus, who was made a little lower than the angels for the suffering of death, crowned with glory and honour; that he by the grace of God should taste death for every man. For it became him, for whom are all things, and by whom are all things, in bringing many sons unto glory, to make the captain of their salvation perfect through sufferings.

Hebrews 2:6-10

We see Jesus Christ, and this brings us into glory and makes rulership our portion. You and I are in charge of running the Universe with Jesus, for we are heirs of God and joint heirs with Christ:

> *And if children, then heirs; heirs of God,*
> *and joint-heirs with Christ; if so be that*
> *we suffer with him, that we may be also*
> *glorified together.*   Romans 8:17

In and through Christ Jesus, we are now in charge. Jesus said that because He has gone to be with the Father, we will now do even greater works than He did in the Earth:

> *Verily, verily, I say unto you, He that*
> *believeth on me, the works that I do*
> *shall he do also; and greater works than*
> *these shall he do; because I go unto my*
> *Father.*   John 14:12

We are to rule the Earth, including its resources. This puts the principalities and powers and hosts of darkness under our authority. This is a commission, an assignment that we are ordained to carry out on Earth. Sadly, many believers don't yet know these truths about the original plan of God for their lives, and Satan thrives on people's ignorance:

> *My people are destroyed for lack of knowledge: because thou hast rejected knowledge, I will also reject thee, that thou shalt be no priest to me: seeing thou hast forgotten the law of thy God, I will also forget thy children.*   Hosea 4:6

When you don't know the truth about your privileges, Satan can easily cheat you out of your place.

> *Now I say, That the heir, as long as he is a child, differeth nothing from a servant, though he be lord of all; but is under tutors and governors until the time appointed of the father. Even so we, when we were children, were in bondage under the elements of the world.*
> Galatians 4:1-3

You may be the heir, but as long as you remain immature in the Spirit, you will easily be cheated. This doesn't have to happen. God's eternal plan does not consider Satan to be a serious obstacle. He cannot stop God, and he also can't stop man. But if you fail to walk in the revelation of God's truth, Satan can easily cheat you out of your rightful place of rulership and dominion.

It is what is written that determines your life, not your experiences. If Abraham had considered his body, he would never have given birth to Isaac. He knew he is in charge, no matter the circumstances.

The same force that caused God to exist made you too, and you are the offspring of the Almighty:

> *And God said, Let us make man in our image, after our likeness: and let them have dominion ... .* Genesis 1:26

No wonder Jesus was able to say with assurance:

> *He that hath seen me hath seen the Father.* John 14:9

> *I and my Father are one.* John 10:30

In Christ, this same truth is now applicable to you. Didn't Jesus say:

He that hateth you hateth me; and he that despiseth you despiseth me; and he that despiseth me despiseth him that sent me.   Luke 10:16

Yes, this is your exalted position. Therefore, you will now be heard. God has given you authority over all sickness and disease. Pain must hear you and obey! Failure must hear you and bow! The future must hear you, including all the storms of life. Jesus said:

For I will give you a mouth and wisdom, which all your adversaries shall not be able to gainsay nor resist. Luke 21:15

Yes, God has given you a mouth and wisdom. Therefore, it is time for you to be *In Charge* in the name of Jesus Christ. This is the message of the book you hold in your hands. Come with me now as we explore our place in redemption and see what we need to do to assume our rightful position and take over in the name of Jesus Christ.

> *And now, brethren, I commend you to God, and to the word of his grace, which is able to build you up, and to give you an inheritance among all them which are sanctified.*   Acts 20:32

Shalom!
Dr. Abiola Idowu

CHAPTER 1

DIVINE LIFTING, YOUR KEY TO RELEVANCE

He [Jesus] replied, "You are permitted to understand the secret of the Kingdom of God. But I use parables for everything I say to outsiders, so that the Scriptures might be fulfilled:

'When they see what I do,
they will learn nothing.
When they hear what I say,
they will not understand.
Otherwise, they will turn to me
and be forgiven.'"

Mark 4:11-12, NLT

God's Kingdom provisions are delivered in mysteries, and as a believer, it is given unto *you* to know the mysteries of the Kingdom of God. The purpose of God's provision is to make your life a wonder to the world so as to humble those who have not known Christ and bring them to Him.

A divine lifting is our heritage in Christ Jesus. We were not designed to live a normal life. In fact, covenant forbids it. To go from being a slave to being prime minister is not natural, but that is what happened to Joseph of old. To become rich after having been considered a reproach to all is not natural, but that is what happened to our father Abraham. What God wrought in Christ when He raised Him from the dead puts us on a whole new level:

> *I also pray that you will understand the incredible greatness of God's power for us who believe him. This is the same mighty power that raised Christ from the dead and seated him in the place of honor at God's right hand in the*

heavenly realms. Now he is far above any ruler or authority or power or leader or anything else — not only in this world but also in the world to come.

Ephesians 1:19-21, NLT

Jesus didn't just die and then rise to life again; through His death and resurrection God was working out something for the Church. As a result, the key to being in charge is now with you:

Now I say to you that you are Peter (which means "rock"), and upon this rock I will build my church, and all the powers of hell will not conquer it. And I will give you the keys of the Kingdom of Heaven. Whatever you forbid on earth will be forbidden in heaven, and whatever you permit on earth will be permitted in heaven.

Matthew 16:18-19, NLT

That key Jesus talked about is now with you. Whatever you bind on earth is bound in Heaven. What God did in Christ put you back on the throne. Of course, the devil doesn't want you to see this, and that is why you need an understanding heart:

> *The people who sat in darkness*
> *have seen a great light.*
> *And for those who lived in the land*
> *where death casts its shadow,*
> *a light has shined.*
>
> Matthew 4:16, NLT

> *That the communication of thy faith may become effectual by the acknowl-edging of every good thing which is in you in Christ Jesus.* Philemon 1:6

This means that for you to remain in the same position year after year is wrong. It may not be a sin, but you are being robbed of your rightful role. God's plans for your life is to take you *"from glory to glory"* (2 Corinthians 3:18). The King is telling you that it is time for advancement:

The LORD our God spake unto us in Horeb, saying, Ye have dwelt long enough in this mount.

Deuteronomy 1:6

And what I say unto you I say unto all … .

Mark 13:37

Kingdom lifting never ends. It is progressive and will continue until we see the Lord in Glory. It's like the waves of the sea; before one ends, another one is forming to take its place.

The example God showed us through the life of Abraham is proof that you cannot end your journey without becoming an influence for the Kingdom:

Hearken to me, ye that follow after righteousness, ye that seek the LORD: look unto the rock whence ye are hewn, and to the hole of the pit whence ye are digged. Look unto Abraham your father, and unto Sarah that bare you: for I called him alone, and blessed him, and increased him. For the LORD shall comfort Zion: he will comfort all her waste places; and he will make her wilderness like Eden, and her desert like the garden of the LORD; joy and gladness shall be found therein, thanksgiving, and the voice of melody. Isaiah 51:1-3

You were created to make a global impact by means of the divine hand of God upon your life, and if God has a plan, nothing can stop that plan—except you. Never forget that it's your value that determines your impact, and God has already added value to you. Jesus said:

Verily, verily, I say unto you, He that believeth on me, the works that I do shall he do also; and greater works than these shall he do; because I go unto my Father. John 14:12

It's your time to rise.

Two things are forever hungry in life, and their strength determines who you feed.

Either you feed your faith or you feed your fear. When you feed your faith, you experience supernatural lifting. When you feed your fear, you wither and die.

Never forget that divine lifting is not your idea; it's God's will and purpose. Your agreement just brings it to fruition:

> *He shall cause them that come of Jacob to take root: Israel shall blossom and bud, and fill the face of the world with fruit.* Isaiah 27:6

There is a glory moving in the Earth right now. Don't hide from it. Plug yourself in to the stream of God's glory, and you will never be disappointed.

Here are some important principles to remember:

1. Refuse to hide
2. Don't Think Small or You Will Remain Small
3. The Mystery of the Anointing Oil
4. Activate Your Healing by Faith

1. REFUSE TO HIDE

Life may not treat you the way you want it to, but you are given authority to subdue and dominate regardless. Whatever comes to you, and whatever suggestions the situations of life make, refuse to hide. Instead of listening to your situations or circumstances, rule them. God's Word says:

> *There hath no temptation taken you but such as is common to man: but God is faithful, who will not suffer you to be tempted above that ye are able; but will with the temptation also make a way to escape, that ye may be able to bear it.*
> 1 Corinthians 10:13

What you are experiencing is common to man, and it cannot dominate you. You are the one God put in charge and the one Heaven recognizes. Many have forgotten that God sees the future from the past, and He is leading you in spite of your weaknesses and fears. He is encouraging you to trust Him so that He can perfect everything about you.

When God sent the prophet Samuel to anoint Saul, Saul was hiding. Why? Because Saul depended on himself, thinking that his ability was what was needed for his lifting. But, no, it was God's grace that he needed:

> *Therefore they enquired of the LORD further, if the man should yet come thither. And the LORD answered, Behold he hath hid himself among the stuff. And they ran and fetched him thence: and when he stood among the people, he was higher than any of the people from his shoulders and upward.* 1 Samuel 10:22-23

> *And there came an angel of the LORD, and sat under an oak which was in Ophrah, that pertained unto Joash the Abiezrite: and his son Gideon threshed wheat by the winepress, to hide it from the Midianites. And the angel of the LORD appeared unto him, and said unto*

> *him, The* L*ord* *is with thee, thou mighty*
> *man of valour.*   Judges 6:11-12

Each time a word comes to you from the Lord, it is to expose what you have never seen that God Himself has already put in you. It is amazing to see what God sees in us, even when we think nothing is working and we are on the verge of losing hope. God is not moved by our current situation or mood. He speaks based on what He knows we are capable of doing.

God told Abraham, *"I have made you a father of many nations"* (Genesis 17:5, NKJV). What? Didn't God know that Sarah was barren? Of course He knew, but He also knew what He saw in their future, and that was what He declared. Don't be surprised that you are reading this today. It is because of what God has seen that you have not yet seen. Stop hiding, and take your rightful place.

The disciples of Jesus demonstrated a very high level of unbelief after He was crucified. They could not believe that He had risen from the dead:

Still later he appeared to the eleven disciples as they were eating together. He rebuked them for their stubborn unbelief because they refused to believe those who had seen him after he had been raised from the dead.　　Mark 16:14, NLT

Amazingly, Jesus then commissioned these same disciples as His representatives in the Earth:

And then he told them, "Go into all the world and preach the Good News to everyone. Anyone who believes and is baptized will be saved. But anyone who refuses to believe will be condemned."
　　　　　　　　Mark 16:15-16, NLT

You, too, are called to be a trailblazer. It may not seem like that could be true, but it is. The tempo of life changes when you discover the faith God has in you. He has never, even once, doubted that you are able, for He sees Himself in you always.

Many are hiding from destiny because they cannot see the deposit that has been made on the inside of them. Increase Your fellowship with God, and you will make a great discovery.

The fact that you are hiding does not stop God's lifting. He is at work on your behalf even now.

What many people don't realize is that promotion, or lifting, comes with assignment, a responsibility, a service to perform. If you never discover who you are sent to, how can you maximize the grace that brings your promotion? If Moses had just continued sitting on the backside of the desert, nothing would have changed. You, too, can do what you are called to do. You can win this war.

The greatest thing you should always remember is that God is with you. David sang:

> *Yea, though I walk through the valley of the shadow of death, I will fear no evil: for thou art with me; thy rod and thy staff they comfort me.* Psalm 23:4

There can be no failure in the assignment God has given to you and no room for setbacks. He is with you.

When Moses was called, he asked, "Who will I say has sent me to Pharaoh?" (see Exodus 3:13). God responded by giving Moses the most powerful weapon possible against the hosts of Egypt. He told Moses to respond: *I AM hath sent me unto you"* (Exodus 3:14). In the same way, God has given you the authority of the name of Jesus Christ. That name is our strong tower (see Proverbs 18:10), and at that name, *"every knee should bow, of those in heaven, and of those on earth, and of those under the earth"* (Philippians 2:10, NKJV).

Never allow the negative voice of the enemy or your adversaries to overcome the voice of God in your life. Let the voice of the Lord be established in your life, and the voice of the enemy will disappear.

God will never destroy you just because you are afraid. He will encourage you and help you. He has already invested in you:

> *Then Samuel said to all the people, "This*
> *is the man the* LORD *has chosen as your*
> *king. No one in all Israel is like him!"*
> *And all the people shouted, "Long live*
> *the king!"*　　　1 Samuel 10:24, NLT

This was Saul's introduction to the people, and God was speaking based on His investment, not Saul's present actions. Far too often we have made rules in church that have killed the giants in us. Wake up! It's your turn to rise.

2. DON'T THINK SMALL OR YOU WILL REMAIN SMALL

You can't be small on the inside and produce great results, for your thinking affects your living. King Saul's great flaw was small thinking. Because the people were honoring him, he allowed their voices to determine his actions. The result was that he was rejected as captain over God's people. Kings can't be using baby bottles. Woe to the land whose king is a child!

Now I say, That the heir, as long as he is a child, differeth nothing from a servant, though he be lord of all. Galatians 4:1

Saul's end was not at all glorious:

Then Samuel said to Saul, "Stop! Listen to what the LORD told me last night!"

"What did he tell you?" Saul asked.

And Samuel told him, "Although you may think little of yourself, are you not the leader of the tribes of Israel? The LORD has anointed you king of Israel. And the LORD sent you on a mission and told you, 'Go and completely destroy the sinners, the Amalekites, until they are all dead.' Why haven't you obeyed the LORD? Why did you rush for the plunder and do what was evil in the LORD's sight?"

"But I did obey the LORD," Saul insisted. "I carried out the mission he gave me. I brought back King Agag, but I destroyed everyone else. Then my troops brought in the best of the sheep, goats, cattle, and plunder to sacrifice to

the LORD your God in Gilgal."
But Samuel replied,
"What is more pleasing to the LORD:
  your burnt offerings and sacrifices
  or your obedience to his voice?
Listen! Obedience is better than sacrifice,
  and submission is better than offering
the fat of rams.
Rebellion is as sinful as witchcraft,
  and stubbornness as bad as worship-
ing idols.
So because you have rejected the command of the LORD,
  he has rejected you as king."

Numbers 13:33, NLT

How do you see yourself? Your promotion cannot be put into motion until you change the way your think about yourself.

Don't be discouraged! There is something in you, no matter how small it may appear. Make use of it! Engage it, and God will multiply it.

Your spirit is from God, and it knows and believes the truth, but if your mouth deceives your spirit, it can bring your spirit to confusion:

> *If you claim to be religious but don't control your tongue, you are fooling yourself, and your religion is worthless.* James 1:26, NLT

If what you are saying is contrary to your heart or your spirit, no wonder you are confused. That is why you look smaller than God's intention. You must begin to speak out loud what God says concerning you:

Jesus said:

> *Don't you believe that I am in the Father and the Father is in me? The words I speak are not my own, but my Father who lives in me does his work through me.* John 14:10, NLT

The Father who dwells in you will do the work. Yes, there is a need for divine lifting. Why? Because man was divinely down. Through his sin, he had lost his glory and splendor:

> *For everyone has sinned; we all fall short
> of God's glorious standard.*
>
> Romans 3:23, NLT

We all lost the glory, and with it, we lost our defense. The glory is the power that puts us into the realm of wonders. That's what we lost. Glory is the full manifestation of the essence of creating or making a thing, and now it's back:

> *And the glory which thou [Father]
> gavest me [Jesus] I have given them
> [those who believe on Me]; that they
> may be one, even as we are one.*
>
> John 17:22

You cannot have the glory and not be in charge.

A total turnaround begins when you believe what God believes about you and you begin to take steps in that direction. Never forget: it was not your efforts that saved you. No, it was His grace. Your faith, however, is needed because you must acknowledge His effort over you:

For by grace are ye saved through faith; and that not of yourselves: it is the gift of God: not of works, lest any man should boast. Ephesians 2:8-9

Your lifting is a result of the effort of God to put you on top. Like David, God found you:

I have found David my servant; with my holy oil have I anointed him: with whom my hand shall be established: mine arm also shall strengthen him. The enemy shall not exact upon him; nor the son of wickedness afflict him. And I will beat down his foes before his face, and plague them that hate him.
Psalm 89:20-23

Jesus said:

You did not choose Me, but I chose you and appointed you that you should go and bear fruit, and that your fruit should remain, that whatever you ask

> *the Father in My name He may give*
> *you.*   John 15:16, NKJV

God chose you for results, for fruit, and you cannot escape His lifting because His choice never fails:

> *Declaring the end from the beginning,*
> *and from ancient times the things that*
> *are not yet done, saying, My counsel*
> *shall stand, and I will do all my plea-*
> *sure.*   Isaiah 46:10

> *For I know the thoughts that I think*
> *toward you, saith the LORD, thoughts*
> *of peace, and not of evil, to give you an*
> *expected end.*   Jeremiah 29:11

It is amazing when we come to understand that what God sees in us is completely different from what men see. God saw a king in David when even his parents couldn't see it. God saw a nation in Abraham and a warrior in Gideon. These things did not seem possible, but they all came to pass just as God had said. Today He sees a victor, a winner, in you, and it's time that you began to cooperate with what He has already seen in you. He said:

> *But ye are a chosen generation, a royal priesthood, an holy nation, a peculiar people; that ye should shew forth the praises of him who hath called you out of darkness into his marvellous light.*
>
> 1 Peter 2:9

If God has seen in you a royal priesthood and a peculiar person, it should not be a surprise to you that you have been chosen in the name of Jesus Christ. Now, it is obeying His commandments that will make you a commander. Nothing will stop you because you have been sent to fulfill a destiny:

> *And the LORD shall make thee the head, and not the tail; and thou shalt be above only, and thou shalt not be beneath; if that thou hearken unto the command-ments of the LORD thy God, which I*

> *command thee this day, to observe and*
> *to do them.* Deuteronomy 28:13

This makes me see that divine lifting begins with the discovery of your purpose. When purpose is discovered, living is simplified. If you don't know where you're going, how will you know when you get there? If you don't know your purpose, how can you understand what to do with your life—even when opportunities arise?

Proverbs declares:

> *Where there is no vision, the people perish: but he that keepeth the law, happy*
> *is he.* Proverbs 29:18

People don't perish because of the devil; they perish because of a lack of vision. When purpose is lost, death becomes attractive, for there seems to be nothing to live for.

Paul was traveling on a ship that was threatened with destruction in a severe storm. Still, he said to his fellow passengers and the crew of the ship:

I exhort you to be of good cheer: for there shall be no loss of any man's life among you, but of the ship. Acts 27:22

How could he be so positive and cheerful? He explained:

For there stood by me this night the angel of God, whose I am, and whom I serve, saying, Fear not, Paul; thou must be brought before Caesar: and, lo, God hath given thee all them that sail with thee. Wherefore, sirs, be of good cheer: for I believe God, that it shall be even as it was told me. Acts 27:23-25

In other words, "Don't worry about this storm, for I have a purpose. I must testify before Caesar." In this way, Paul cheapened the power of death. How? Because he knew he was on a mission. And you, too, are on a mission. God has sent you to be His witness on Earth in the twenty-first century.

If you lack an understanding of your mission, you begin to lose confidence in the one who sent you. Stop struggling with your purpose. It came with the product, and a product is never produced without an intention on the part of the manufacturer. It is his or her dream come to pass. You came here by the determinate counsel of God Himself, and He has provided all it will take for you to make an impact.

The highest way of living is living according to God's plans. He establishes those plans and then sows them into your life through your thoughts and dreams:

> *The thoughts of the righteous are right: but the counsels of the wicked are deceit.* Proverbs 12:5

Those thoughts are being fired into your spirit so that you can enjoy divine providence:

> *Faithful is he that calleth you, who also will do it.* 1 Thessalonians 5:24

*For it is God which worketh in you both
to will and to do of his good pleasure.*
Philippians 2:13

You can overcome every limitation because Heaven is backing you up. You can
remove every blockage because no one can
stop the One who sent you:

*But unto you that fear my name shall
the Sun of righteousness arise with healing in his wings; and ye shall go forth,
and grow up as calves of the stall.*
Malachi 4:2

I'm not suggesting that the enemy will
not be angry about your success. What
I *am* suggesting is that he cannot stop
it—never:

*Behold, I send an Angel before thee, to
keep thee in the way, and to bring thee
into the place which I have prepared.*
Exodus 23:20

> *Thou preparest a table before me in the presence of mine enemies: thou anointest my head with oil; my cup runneth over.* Psalm 23:5

All it takes to live a life of victory and results on Earth is faith in God and in His Word:

> *But without faith it is impossible to please him: for he that cometh to God must believe that he is, and that he is a rewarder of them that diligently seek him.* Hebrews 11:6

The power of God is always available to you, and the blessing of God and His glory are always there. But faith is the activator:

> *Moreover whom he did predestinate, them he also called: and whom he called, them he also justified: and whom he justified, them he also glorified.* Romans 8:30

You have no issues with God's glory, His calling, or His justification. All that is required to activate them is faith. Jesus said it like this to two blind men: *"Do you believe that I am able to do this?"* (Matthew 9:28, NKJV). That was all that was required. The rest is testimony:

> *Jesus said to him, "If you can believe, all things are possible to him who believes."* Mark 9:23, NKJV

No matter what, don't ever say what the devil has asked you to say. It won't work. He may wrap his words with facts, but you must stand on God's truth:

> *Now it happened, on a certain day, that He got into a boat with His disciples. And He said to them, "Let us cross over to the other side of the lake." And they launched out. But as they sailed He fell asleep. And a windstorm came down on the lake, and they were filling with water, and were in jeopardy. And they*

came to Him and awoke Him, saying,
"Master, Master, we are perishing!"
Then He arose and rebuked the wind
and the raging of the water. And they
ceased, and there was a calm. But He
said to them, "Where is your faith?"
And they were afraid, and marveled,
saying to one another, "Who can this
be? For He commands even the winds
and water, and they obey Him!"

Luke 8:22-25, NKJV

The devil had stolen the faith of these disciples, and they were speaking against Jesus' word. There is a sword in your mouth (see Revelation 1:16). Use it now!

3. THE MYSTERY OF THE ANOINTING OIL

One of the major truths that sets you on top is the mystery of the anointing oil. This is the Kingdom instrument that humiliates the adversary and lifts you up. Anointed oil brings the ability and the energy of Heaven upon humans:

> *Then Samuel took the horn of oil, and anointed him in the midst of his brethren: and the Spirit of the LORD came upon David from that day forward.*
>
> 1 Samuel 16:13

After the anointing oil was poured on David, and the Spirit of God came upon him, he killed a lion and a bear, and then he killed the giant Goliath. This was not natural; it was a divine arrangement.

Throughout the Bible we see that when the oil of God came upon a person, advancement came with it. You are about to overtake your classmates or work mates.

The hand of the Lord came upon Elijah, and he outran the chariots of King Ahab:

> *And Ahab rode, and went to Jezreel. And the hand of the LORD was on Elijah; and he girded up his loins, and ran before Ahab to the entrance of Jezreel.* 1 Kings 18:45-46

The anointing oil of the New Testament has the same power:

> *Is any sick among you? let him call for the elders of the church; and let them pray over him, anointing him with oil in the name of the Lord: and the prayer of faith shall save the sick, and the Lord shall raise him up; and if he have com-mitted sins, they shall be forgiven him.*
> James 5:14-15

It was the same oil. Jesus sent His disciples out two by two with that same oil, and they had power to perform miracles:

> *And they went out, and preached that men should repent. And they cast out many devils, and anointed with oil many that were sick, and healed them.*
> Mark 6:12-13

As you are anointed, every chain will drop and every oppression will give way in the name of Jesus Christ:

So shall they fear the name of the LORD from the west, and his glory from the rising of the sun. When the enemy shall come in like a flood, the Spirit of the LORD shall lift up a standard against him.   Isaiah 59:19

4. ACTIVATE YOUR HEALING BY FAITH

When faith comes alive, victory is obtained immediately. This is called agreement with God:

She [the woman with the issue of blood] said, If I may touch but his clothes, I shall be whole. And straightway the fountain of her blood was dried up; and she felt in her body that she was healed of that plague.   Mark 5:28-29

Divine lifting is not a function of wishing. No, it is an operation of the faith of God:

And Jesus said unto them, ... Verily I say unto you, If ye have faith as a grain of mustard seed, ye shall say unto this mountain, Remove hence to yonder place; and it shall remove; and nothing shall be impossible unto you.

Matthew 17:20

Believing the Word will move anything out of your way. The Bible says, *"Nothing shall be impossible unto you."* When you speak this, you are not reasoning with your head, but with the power of the Scriptures. You must agree that God knows better than you, and this promise is from His Love Book. He said:

Arise, shine; for thy light is come, and the glory of the LORD is risen upon thee.

Isaiah 60:1

God isn't delaying your lifting; it is your faith that determines what you get or don't get:

Withhold not good from them to whom it is due, when it is in the power of thine hand to do it. Say not unto thy neighbour, Go, and come again, and to morrow I will give; when thou hast it by thee. Proverbs 3:27-28

Don't say to your neighbor, "Come back tomorrow!" Stop trying to perform. Let the performance be God's, and you just enjoy the show:

And blessed is she that believed: for there shall be a performance of those things which were told her from the Lord. Luke 1:45

There is nothing in the dark but the lies of the enemy. There is nothing remaining in his hand but fear, and if you fear, you have enabled him:

But whoso hearkeneth unto me shall dwell safely, and shall be quiet from fear of evil. Proverbs 1:33

In righteousness shalt thou be established: thou shalt be far from oppression;

> *for thou shalt not fear: and from terror;*
> *for it shall not come near thee.*
>
> Isaiah 54:14

Good News that does not include healing and deliverance is incomplete.

> *Now after that John was put in prison,*
> *Jesus came into Galilee, preaching the*
> *gospel of the kingdom of God.*
>
> Mark 1:14

> *And there was in their synagogue a man*
> *with an unclean spirit; and he cried out,*
> *saying, Let us alone; what have we to do*
> *with thee, thou Jesus of Nazareth? art*
> *thou come to destroy us? I know thee*
> *who thou art, the Holy One of God.*
> *And Jesus rebuked him, saying, Hold*
> *thy peace, and come out of him.*
>
> Mark 1:23-25

> *And he said unto them, Let us go into*
> *the next towns, that I may preach there*
> *also: for therefore came I forth.*
>
> Mark 1:38

If He came for this, you are free today:

And when Peter saw it, he answered unto the people, Ye men of Israel, why marvel ye at this? or why look ye so earnestly on us, as though by our own power or holiness we had made this man to walk? The God of Abraham, and of Isaac, and of Jacob, the God of our fathers, hath glorified his Son Jesus; whom ye delivered up, and denied him in the presence of Pilate, when he was determined to let him go. Acts 3:12-13

Understand this truth: sickness and diseases do not come from God. They are from the devil:

How God anointed Jesus of Nazareth with the Holy Ghost and with power: who went about doing good, and healing all that were oppressed of the devil; for God was with him. Acts 10:38

> *And ought not this woman, being a daughter of Abraham, whom Satan hath bound, lo, these eighteen years, be loosed from this bond on the sabbath day?*
>
> Luke 13:16

And if these are from the devil, then God's children should not have to bear them. We don't want Satan's "stuff" in our lives. If Jesus was approved by miracles, then His approval must manifest in the lives of His children today:

> *Ye men of Israel, hear these words; Jesus of Nazareth, a man approved of God among you by miracles and wonders and signs, which God did by him in the midst of you, as ye yourselves also know.*
>
> Acts 2:22

Jesus was approved and endorsed because of the miracles He did, and these must still be in evidence today. Many Christians never see miracles because God doesn't do things by preference but by principle. He loves you, but your response goes a long way. What can you do?

1. **Serve the Lord**: Your response to God's love must be service. If you fail to serve Him, then you become a slave to Satan:

Know ye not, that to whom ye yield yourselves servants to obey, his servants ye are to whom ye obey; whether of sin unto death, or of obedience unto righteousness? But God be thanked, that ye were the servants of sin, but ye have obeyed from the heart that form of doctrine which was delivered you.

Romans 6:16-17

In Exodus 23:25-26, there is a guarantee that God will preserve your health when you serve Him, and He cannot deny Himself or His Word. Hezekiah cheated death through service. He had served God his whole life and then got very sick. Was this the way God rewarded service? He seemed to be at the point of death, but God added fifteen years to his life (see Isaiah 38:1-5).

Never forget that God is a jealous God and can't stand you putting anything before Him. When you are no more in His service, your name is missing from His payroll:

> *And they shall be mine, saith the L*ORD *of hosts, in that day when I make up my jewels; and I will spare them, as a man spareth his own son that serveth him. Then shall ye return, and discern between the righteous and the wicked, between him that serveth God and him that serveth him not.* Malachi 3:17-18

> *Because thou servedst not the L*ORD *thy God with joyfulness, and with gladness of heart, for the abundance of all things; therefore shalt thou serve thine enemies which the L*ORD *shall send against thee, in hunger, and in thirst, and in naked-ness, and in want of all things: and he shall put a yoke of iron upon thy neck, until he have destroyed thee.*
> Deuteronomy 28:47-48

Serve God with your time, your money, your gifts, your talents, and your body. Serve Him with all that you have, and He will build a hedge around you. That's exactly what happened to Job:

And the LORD *said unto Satan, Hast thou considered my servant Job, that there is none like him in the earth, a perfect and an upright man, one that feareth God, and escheweth evil? Then Satan answered the* LORD, *and said, Doth Job fear God for nought? Hast not thou made an hedge about him, and about his house, and about all that he hath on every side? thou hast blessed the work of his hands, and his substance is increased in the land.* Job 1:8-10

You serve God by loving Him, loving His Word, loving His house, loving His people, and winning others to Him. You cannot love God without winning souls for Him.

Do you want miracles? Then go for souls, and you will see God's response in your personal life. Jesus taught:

> *And as ye go, preach, saying, The kingdom of heaven is at hand. Heal the sick, cleanse the lepers, raise the dead, cast out devils: freely ye have received, freely give.*
> Matthew 10:7-8

2. **Use the name of Jesus Christ:** Using Jesus' name is not an act of faith; it's an act of understanding. It is authority, it is taking possession. God gave us that name just as surely as we have arms and legs. That name is our possession.

In Acts 3:6 (NLT), Peter said, *"I don't have any silver or gold for you. But I'll give you what I have. In the name of Jesus Christ the Nazarene, get up and walk!"* He possessed that name and now he put a demand on that name. Why? This name has everything in it, and your understanding of that fact makes it work for you. No devil and no pain can stand before that name. Every knee must bow before it. So, use it:

And being found in appearance as a man, He [Jesus] humbled Himself and became obedient to the point of death, even the death of the cross. Therefore God also has highly exalted Him and given Him the name which is above every name, that at the name of Jesus every knee should bow, of those in heaven, and of those on earth, and of those under the earth, and that every tongue should confess that Jesus Christ is Lord, to the glory of God the Father. Philippians 2:8-11, NKJV

Using the name of Jesus, take authority over cancer, diabetes, and paralysis. Let His name fight your every battle.

Understand that the name will not use itself; you must use it. And you don't need any special faith to use it. You would never ask God for faith to use the key to your house. No, all you need is to recognize your key from the bunch of keys and then place it in the lock and turn it. It isn't even something you have to think about. It's effortless.

Jesus has already said to us:

> *You can ask for anything in my name, and I will do it, so that the Son can bring glory to the Father. Yes, ask me for anything in my name, and I will do it!* John 14:13-14, NLT

Why is the name of Jesus so powerful? This name is all that counts in Heaven. It opens every door to us and closes every gate to the enemy. If you hold that key, you need not ask for faith to use it. Take that name and go humiliate sickness and diseases now:

> *When the seventy-two disciples returned, they joyfully reported to him, "Lord, even the demons obey us when we use your name!"* Luke 10:17, NLT

Judas was there among them, as was Thomas, and they all returned with this common testimony. Now it's your turn to do wonders in Jesus' name. Use it in the following way:

Father, in the name of Jesus Christ, the job I was meant to have is given me now in the name of Jesus Christ, that I might prosper and bless Your Kingdom.

Father, in the name of Jesus Christ, I demand that angels go before me today. I receive unusual favor, and my lifting is established in Jesus' name.

Father, in the name of Jesus Christ, I demand that this pain leave now. Whatever has come into my body in the form of sickness and diseases, I demand it to leave now in the name of Jesus Christ. Thank You, Lord. It is gone in Jesus' name!

Why can you do all of this? Because you are now *In Charge!*

CHAPTER 2

UNWRAPPING YOUR HERITAGE OF FREEDOM

So Christ has truly set us free. Now make sure that you stay free, and don't get tied up again in slavery to the law.
Galatians 5:1, NLT

Freedom is not just an escape from demonic activities or a rescue from bondage. Freedom is living for what you were created for without any hinderance.

You were created for a serious purpose with a very deep intention from the heart of our Father God, and you are now living to fulfill your purpose in life without limitations. That is the essence of life, and that is the reason for living. If God's program and promises are to be fulfilled, you must be free.

The sound of freedom was so clearly echoed for Adam in the garden, *"for every tree of the garden you may freely eat"* (Genesis 2:16, NKJV). But with all that God put together for man, man failed because he had his own mind, and it was against God's plan. The result was that he lost everything, including his freedom.

It is not Satan who has the power to put man in bondage but, rather, man's own porous thinking that permits the enemy's entrance. Adam trusted the lies of the enemy more than His Father's love. The moment you think God doesn't love you as much as He said in His Word, your freedom will slip from your hands. When you don't appreciate that God's Word is His plan and purpose, you give the devil a foothold in your life.

Giving us His power and authority is not a problem for God. He is ready and willing to lavish these on His children, but you changing your mind and agreeing with God is where the foundation of freedom lies. This is where the renewing of your mind comes in (see Romans 12:2).

God parted the sea and destroyed Pharaoh for the children of Israel, but He could not change their wrong thinking. They had been delivered from Egypt and slavery, but Egypt and slavery were still in them, and when anything did not go as they had hoped, they were quick to say, "Let's go back to Egypt." Strangely, they remembered the leeks and garlic they had eaten there, but they did not remember the hardships and severe oppression they had suffered there. There is no freedom without right thinking!

The King James Version of the Bible renders Galatians 5:1 like this:

> *Stand fast therefore in the liberty wherewith Christ hath made us free, and be not entangled again with the yoke of bondage.*

If you don't stand on the Word of God, you will hinder the flow of His blessings.

Freedom is what every human on Earth longs for. Everyone—man or woman, boy or girl—wants to fulfill their dreams and aspirations. They want to be in control of their circumstances. This is how they were created to function. When that ability is not there, we call it *bondage*, and all bondage must be broken.

There is a promised land for you, but you must know that it's yours and that no devil can stop you from getting there. Why? Because God is with you, and you are filled with the Holy Spirit who knows how to get the job done.

God is omniscient, omnipotent, and all the rest, but nothing moves in your life without your will being involved:

> *These are the generations of the heavens and of the earth when they were created, in the day that the LORD God made the earth and the heavens, and every plant of the field before it was in the earth, and every herb of the field before it grew: for the LORD God had not*

caused it to rain upon the earth, and there was not a man to till the ground.
                                    Genesis 2:4-5

It had never rained before. Why? Because the managers were not there yet. When the managers got into place, things began to work. Maybe what you are believing God for is already in your house, and all you need to do is to change your thinking in order to see it activated.

You and I are in a business with God:

> *For we are labourers together with God: ye are God's husbandry, ye are God's building.* 1 Corinthians 3:9

The resources are here. Therefore it is time for you and me to start managing this Earth. After all, God has placed us *In Charge.*

It's easier and cheaper to be managed than it is to manage. This is why many are settling for being managed, even Christian believers, because they don't want to take responsibility for managing.

Freedom is not throwing off some restriction; it's not doing whatever you want to do without accountability. True freedom demands great responsibility and accountability, a spirit of stewardship, dependability, maturity, wisdom, and character. It is better to be in slavery than to desire freedom without responsibility and the intention to make an impact. This just leads to depression and frustration. You cannot remain in bondage once you have discovered who you are in Christ and have determined to be that person.

Too often, when we think about freedom, we think of physical freedom. But, no! That's not it. That is called deliverance. However, you can be delivered and still not be free. True freedom is in the mind, and you are free in your mind when you are thinking the truth.

You can be healed and still not be free. What God's Word says about healing and health is completely different from experiencing true freedom in Christ. You may have been delivered and healed, but now you need to be free by having an understanding of what Christ has done for you on the cross regarding your health.

You were born into freedom, and freedom was the basis for Creation. Therefore, if you don't experience true freedom, you get depressed. A lack of freedom is contrary to your destiny, and the pursuit of freedom is a natural trait of humanity.

God is not partial to anyone. Each of us came equipped with all that was required to be great:

> *Blessed are the meek: for they shall inherit the earth.* Matthew 5:5

The difference between the managed and those who manage is that the manager has discovered within him- or herself the resources and the ability and has taken a step of faith (even when it did not make any sense) to fulfill his or her calling in life. The managed are still looking for a day when everything will magically fall in line. That's a tragic mistake. Go for it now! This is your season!

Here are some guidelines to help you reach your goal:

1. **Understand that you have authority and you are also under authority:** The mindset of "what will be will be" is a slavery mentality. Instead, you must think: What would have been can be changed:

> *And God said, Let us make man in our image, after our likeness: and let them have dominion over the fish of the sea, and over the fowl of the air, and over the cattle, and over all the earth, and over every creeping thing that creepeth upon the earth.*   Genesis 1:26

Your arrival on the scene as a redeemed child of God put you in a place of authority and royalty—if you will just recognize it and use it:

> *And they sung a new song, saying, Thou art worthy to take the book, and to open the seals thereof: for thou wast slain, and hast redeemed us to God by*

thy blood out of every kindred, and tongue, and people, and nation; and hast made us unto our God kings and priests: and we shall reign on the earth.

Revelation 5:9-10

Again I say unto you, That if two of you shall agree on earth as touching any thing that they shall ask, it shall be done for them of my Father which is in heaven. For where two or three are gathered together in my name, there am I in the midst of them.

Matthew 18:19-20

Your jurisdiction covers the entire Earth. It is not enough to know that you have authority; you must know Who gave you that authority and why.

The moment you are made a manager or supervisor of any company, you are then expected to take charge and start giving orders. Well, God has ordained you to manage this earthly realm, and you can do this in and through the name of Jesus Christ.

When you begin to use this authority, that is true freedom.

You have nothing to fear. There is Someone backing you up each time you declare His counsel in your territory. When facing Pharaoh's armies at the Red Sea, Moses said to the people of Israel:

> *Fear ye not, stand still, and see the salvation of the* Lord, *which he will shew to you to day: for the Egyptians whom ye have seen to day, ye shall see them again no more for ever. The* Lord *shall fight for you, and ye shall hold your peace.* Exodus 14:13-14

Then Moses stretched out his rod, and the sea parted. Why? Because he was under authority, and he was called to manage.

Never forget: you are not empowered just for your own benefit. It is for the sake of the Kingdom, to spread the Kingdom all over the Earth. If that is not done, your freedom will be hindered.

2. **Understand your value and what you are capable of doing:** What you don't value diminishes. What you carry is the reason for your impact. You and I are to team up with God in fulfilling His eternal agenda, and we have all that it takes. God Himself put it there:

> *Behold the fowls of the air: for they sow not, neither do they reap, nor gather into barns; yet your heavenly Father feedeth them. Are ye not much better than they? Which of you by taking thought can add one cubit unto his stature? And why take ye thought for raiment? Consider the lilies of the field, how they grow; they toil not, neither do they spin: and yet I say unto you, That even Solomon in all his glory was not arrayed like one of these.* Matthew 6:26-29

It's amazing what we can learn from birds. The blame game and a lack of self-control destroyed the destiny of the first Adam, and that is the foundation of irresponsibility. The world owes you nothing. You owe the world your input, for you were designed to dress and keep this planet:

> And the LORD God took the man, and put him into the garden of Eden to dress it and to keep it.   Genesis 2:15

Faithful stewardship is the key to mastering your calling. What you do with what God has put inside you is the key to your freedom. His mandate has never changed:

> And God blessed them, and God said unto them, Be fruitful, and multiply, and replenish the earth, and subdue it: and have dominion over the fish of the sea, and over the fowl of the air, and over every living thing that moveth upon the earth.   Genesis 1:28

God has never changed this commission in spite of the Fall of man. It still remains intact, and that's why Heaven is looking to you to act:

> *And I say also unto thee, That thou art Peter, and upon this rock I will build my church; and the gates of hell shall not prevail against it.* Matthew 16:18

3. **Don't look for a job; discover your life's work:** The reason many are frustrated is that they are just looking for job. A job will pay the bills, but what of the work you were born to do? That is what will satisfy you. Jesus said:

> *I have meat to eat that ye know not of.*
> John 4:32

> *My meat is to do the will of him that sent me, and to finish his work.* John 4:34

Doing God's will brings total satisfaction, and if you are not doing that, you are in disobedience. Your potential is to be found in your work for Him, not necessarily in an earthly job.

With your work, you are to produce results. God said, *"Be fruitful,"* showing that
you carry a seed within you that has the potential of bearing fruit for everyone around
you. When they see your fruits, they will be
gathered to you:

> *And God said, Let the earth bring forth
> grass, the herb yielding seed, and the
> fruit tree yielding fruit after his kind,
> whose seed is in itself, upon the earth:
> and it was so.* Genesis 1:11

Everything and everyone has seed. This
is a gift from God. But in order to bear fruit
that seed must be properly planted and
properly cultivated. A seed that is never
planted is just a seed. It will produce nothing. An idea God places in you cannot bless
humanity until you take the proper steps.

If an idea comes from your mind, it is no
bigger than you, but if it comes from God,
it has unlimited potential.

When God created the Heaven and the
Earth, He did not create tables and chairs.

He created trees and hid tables and chairs inside of them. Adam had to get them out.

Mountains and hills were not created just for fun. Inside those hills are potential cars and airplanes because the raw materials for them are there, just waiting to be extracted and put to good use. You might say, "But Bishop Idowu, I can't do that." Yes, you can. God knew all that Adam could do long before Adam himself knew it, and He brought all the animals to Adam to name them. Why would God do that? Because He wanted to show this man what he was capable of.

The thoughts and ideas that come to your mind could be for new inventions, things not yet discovered. If God entrusted you with those ideas, He knew you could handle them. Do what Adam did. Give that thing a name. I am convinced that this is why so many people are restless and frustrated. Their soul is crying out for true freedom.

Until you challenge the status quo, you will be forever tied to a stake. Until you shout, "Enough is enough," you will never change your status in life. Break free!

Nothing is permitted to hold you bound, for you are in the class of divinity:

> *And God said, Let us make man in our image, after our likeness: and let them have dominion over the fish of the sea, and over the fowl of the air, and over the cattle, and over all the earth, and over every creeping thing that creepeth upon the earth.* Genesis 1:26

> *Then said Jesus to them again, Peace be unto you: as my Father hath sent me, even so send I you.* John 20:21

Too many have conditioned their mind to what is around them and not to what God says in His Word. We have misunderstood our calling and our assignment because of traditions and religious backgrounds. This includes the culture we learned from fallen Adam. Consequently, we struggle to take the new approach Jesus Christ introduced to us because it is not popular, and this is not how the rest of the world does things. We foolishly choose to pursue things based on the world's view. Why? Because that is what we have learned in school. Myles Munroe has said, "Condition determines conduct until it is interrupted by external force."

Jesus Christ came primarily to open prison doors, and He did that:

> *The people which sat in darkness saw great light; and to them which sat in the region and shadow of death light is sprung up.* Matthew 4:16

However, even though Jesus destroyed prison gates, the prisoners have refused to come out. Why would they do that? They were accustomed to their sufferings and have explanations for everything. I hear people saying, "If you only knew what I've been through." We know, but come out now by believing the truth:

> *The Spirit of the Lord is upon me, because he hath anointed me to preach the gospel to the poor; he hath sent me to*

> *heal the brokenhearted, to preach deliv-*
> *erance to the captives, and recovering of*
> *sight to the blind, to set at liberty them*
> *that are bruised, to preach the acceptable*
> *year of the Lord.* Luke 4:18-19

You may want a certain job or a certain position, but are you willing to change what you
are doing to get it? If not, it won't happen.

Ask God for grace to do what will make
you an influence. The power is already
there. You just need to wake up to it.

It's easy to be a person of no responsibility, and that is why many prefer to be
delivered and not be set free. If other people
must depend on you, you have to raise your
standard. You have to wake up earlier, study
more, and show more commitment. You can
do that because inside of you is the same
Spirit that raised Jesus from the dead. So
what are you still doing in life's graveyard?

> *Awake, awake; put on thy strength, O*
> *Zion; put on thy beautiful garments, O*
> *Jerusalem, the holy city: for henceforth*

there shall no more come into thee the uncircumcised and the unclean. Shake thyself from the dust; arise, and sit down, O Jerusalem: loose thyself from the bands of thy neck, O captive daughter of Zion. Isaiah 52:1-2

Wherefore he saith, Awake thou that sleepest, and arise from the dead, and Christ shall give thee light.
Ephesians 5:14

Stand fast therefore in the liberty wherewith Christ hath made us free, and be not entangled again with the yoke of bondage. Galatians 5:1

We have all been delivered from the power of darkness, and we have been also translated into the Kingdom of Christ:

Who hath delivered us from the power of darkness, and hath translated us into the kingdom of his dear Son.
Colossians 1:13

Because we are filled with the Holy Spirit, we are expected to live a life of daily miracles, but unless and until our minds are renewed and we know the intention of God for our lives, oppression will not stop:

> *When Pharaoh finally let the people go, God did not lead them along the main road that runs through Philistine territory, even though that was the shortest route to the Promised Land. God said, "If the people are faced with a battle, they might change their minds and return to Egypt."* Exodus 13:17, NLT

That is what Paul also revealed about the Church. God's intention is to show principalities and power who He is through the Church:

> *To the intent that now unto the principalities and powers in heavenly places might be known by the church the manifold wisdom of God.* Ephesians 3:10

Stop the oppression and wilderness experience now! You are not the victim; you are a victor. Jesus Christ already paid the price for your freedom.

There is a need to change our ideology, our culture, our language, and wilderness diet and start living like kings in our territory. If you stay too long in one spot, be careful! You might need to change something in your thinking. We were intended to go *"from strength to strength"*:

> *They go from strength to strength, every one of them in Zion appeareth before God.* Psalm 84:7

It has been estimated that the journey the Israelites took from Egypt to the Promised Land should have taken no more than thirty-five days. In reality, it took forty years. Information does not bring transformation without actualization.

There are so many things that we know, and yet we do nothing about them. We continue to propose what might be accomplished and to offer excuses as to why it is not happening. This is crazy! What were these people thinking? How could a journey of thirty-five days take forty years to complete?

God doesn't just want your plan. He calls you to reason with Him (see Isaiah 1:18). The prodigal son *"came to himself"* (Luke 15:17) and realized, "This must not continue, for I have a father who loves me!" Conceive what you are hearing, and you will produce what you are desiring.

Because something is new and great does not guarantee freedom and change if you don't yet know what it's for. You can have a new computer and not know how to maximize its usage.

Now, for the next level agenda:

1. **Determine to change yourself**: God only inspires a change; you are the one who makes the determination. God gives the power, but you execute the authority:

> *No weapon that is formed against thee*
> *shall prosper; and every tongue that shall*

rise against thee in judgment thou shalt condemn. This is the heritage of the servants of the LORD, *and their righteousness is of me, saith the* LORD.   Isaiah 54:17

God has said:

And be not conformed to this world: but be ye transformed by the renewing of your mind, that ye may prove what is that good, and acceptable, and perfect, will of God.   Romans 12:2

Wherefore lay apart all filthiness and superfluity of naughtiness, and receive with meekness the engrafted word, which is able to save your souls.

James 1:21

The law of the LORD *is perfect, converting the soul: the testimony of the* LORD *is sure, making wise the simple.*

Psalm 19:7

The truth is that your spirit has been completely changed and is now in union with

God through our Lord Jesus, but you must work on your mind by feeding it with God's thoughts. Change will never come through what we *feel* but through what we *know*. The reason many of the Israelites were buried in the wilderness was because they devalued God, traded the Promised Land for Egypt, and refused to change their grasshopper mentality. They had to go, and God buried them for the sake of saving others from their polluted way of thinking.

It was not the people who saw themselves as grasshoppers who would take Jericho, Ai, and Canaan. That would have made God look like a liar. Because of His holiness, they had to go. God called them a kingdom of priests; grasshoppers could not take the Promised Land.

Never forget: slaves don't talk back, and they don't think their own thoughts; they only do what their master says. God wasn't about to baby-sit these children in the Promised Land. There the manna ceased, and they started eating the corn of the land:

84

And the manna ceased on the morrow
after they had eaten of the old corn of the
land; neither had the children of Israel
manna any more; but they did eat of the
fruit of the land of Canaan that year.
                                    Joshua 5:12

Now the people were sowing and reaping. Now they were ruling the planet. Now they determined what they wanted to eat based on their tastes, not just on what happened to be available at the moment.

2. **Walk out into your new world of opportunities:** The whole world is at your fingertips in Christ, and you are not limited by any force:

Therefore let no man glory in men. For
all things are your's; whether Paul, or
Apollos, or Cephas, or the world, or life,
or death, or things present, or things to
come; all are your's; and ye are Christ's;
and Christ is God's.
                            1 Corinthians 3:21-23

The Bible says:

With God all things are possible.
Matthew 19:26

In Mark 9:23, Jesus declared:

All things are possible to him that believeth.

Therefore, go forth and break all barriers. Say what you have never said before, and do what you have never done before. Act based on God's promises:

I can do all things through Christ which strengtheneth me.   Philippians 4:13

No weapon that is formed against thee shall prosper; and every tongue that shall rise against thee in judgment thou shalt condemn.   Isaiah 54:17

Greater is he that is in you, than he that is in the world.   1 John 4:4

Many are trapped in their past, they complain a lot about it, and are frustrated and depressed. But God has already moved on. He set a new world above that, so get out of that trap. You are better than that, and this is why you have survived it. Yes, you may have some scars. It's called "experience." You can use those scars to teach others to win in that same area. Instead of being a slave to your past, you can use your past to glorify God and help others avoid life's pitfalls. Paul wrote:

> *Brethren, I count not myself to have apprehended: but this one thing I do, forgetting those things which are behind, and reaching forth unto those things which are before, I press toward the mark for the prize of the high calling of God in Christ Jesus. Let us therefore, as many as be perfect, be thus minded: and if in any thing ye be otherwise minded, God shall reveal even this unto you. Nevertheless, whereto we have already attained, let us walk by the same rule, let us mind the*

same thing. Brethren, be followers to-
gether of me, and mark them which walk
so as ye have us for an ensample.
Philippians 3:13-17

That is why the people you relate with and fellowship with matter so much. Leave the doubters and pouters and join the victorious. God said:

Remember ye not the former things, nei-
ther consider the things of old. Behold, I
will do a new thing; now it shall spring
forth; shall ye not know it? I will even
make a way in the wilderness, and rivers
in the desert. Isaiah 43:18-19

Don't give power to your past; give strength to your future. Stop looking back and move on into your future:

And Jesus said unto him, No man,
having put his hand to the plough, and
looking back, is fit for the kingdom of
God. Luke 9:62

You can now get up from your prostration and become the person you were created to be, and you can do it in Jesus' name. It's time for the next level. Use that name like this:

Father, in the name of Jesus Christ, today I put a total end to every limitation and frustration in my life. I say to every limitation and frustration, "Stop now!" And God's Word declares, *"Affliction shall not rise up the second time"* (Nahum 1:9)!

Father, in the name of Jesus Christ, I decree doors opening for me in diverse places, for You have said, *"The lines are fallen unto me in pleasant places; yea, I have a goodly heritage"* (Psalm 16:6). This promise shall be mine in Jesus' name.

Father, in the name of Jesus, I declare this day complete restoration. Nothing shall fail, and I will achieve success for Your honor and glory.

There is no bondage in God's Kingdom. Every Kingdom citizens is free, but not every citizens stands in the truth. Why? Because of the deception of the enemy. It is up to us to walk in the freedom Christ has provided for us:

> *So Christ has truly set us free. Now make sure that you stay free, and don't get tied up again in slavery to the law.*
> Galatians 5:1, NLT

We are called to glory, and there is no shame here. We are perfectly represented in Heaven, and we are taking our place for Him on Earth:

> *God, for whom and through whom everything was made, chose to bring many children into glory. And it was only right that he should make Jesus, through his suffering, a perfect leader, fit to bring them into their salvation.*
> Hebrews 2:10, NLT

The early Christian didn't just talk about having faith; they acted out the Word of God. Jesus didn't go around telling people that He had faith. He just acted out the Word. He said:

Believest thou not that I am in the Father, and the Father in me? the words that I speak unto you I speak not of myself: but the Father that dwelleth in me, he doeth the works. John 14:10

When ye have lifted up the Son of man, then shall ye know that I am he, and that I do nothing of myself; but as my Father hath taught me, I speak these things. And he that sent me is with me: the Father hath not left me alone; for I do always those things that please him. John 8:28-29

The end of frustration, calamity, sickness, and disease comes when you know the will of God and you act on that will:

For ye have need of patience, that, after ye have done the will of God, ye might receive the promise.   Hebrews 10:36

How dare you talk about weakness when the will of God is strength! How dare you talk about sickness when the will of God is health!

Beloved, I wish above all things that thou mayest prosper and be in health, even as thy soul prospereth.   3 John 2

And the inhabitant shall not say, I am sick: the people that dwell therein shall be forgiven their iniquity. Isaiah 33:24

The will of God is your total peace, and that peace is already with you:

For the mountains shall depart, and the hills be removed; but my kindness shall not depart from thee, neither shall the covenant of my peace be removed, saith the LORD that hath mercy on thee.
Isaiah 54:10

The will of God is the Word of God. He has already said:

My counsel shall stand, and I will do all my pleasure. Isaiah 46:10

Heaven and earth shall pass away, but my words shall not pass away.
Matthew 24:35

So shall my word be that goeth forth out of my mouth: it shall not return unto me void, but it shall accomplish that which I please, and it shall prosper in the thing whereto I sent it. For ye shall go out with joy, and be led forth with peace: the mountains and the hills shall break forth before you into singing, and all the trees of the field shall clap their hands. Isaiah 55:11-12

Think about it this way: The will of Toyota is making a vehicle that will take you where you want to go. To achieve that goal, they put together the right electrical, mechanical, and computer parts. To use that vehicle, you don't have to understand everything that has been put together, but you must obey some basic principles. You must start the engine (or motor), you must engage the transmission, and you must press the accelerator. When you have taken these steps, the vehicle starts to move.

It is the same with God. Press His Word in faith and the Word delivers its intention. Healing comes. Breakthroughs come. This is what John 15:7 says:

> *If ye abide in me, and my words abide in you, ye shall ask what ye will, and it shall be done unto you.*

Total freedom and healing come with the Word of the living God:

> *And this is the confidence that we have in him, that, if we ask any thing according to his will, he heareth us.*
>   1 John 5:14

The easiest way to avoid living in darkness is to walk in the light. God has promised:

With long life will I satisfy him, and shew him my salvation.   Psalm 91:16

That is God's will. If Jesus took our infirmities upon Himself and bore them on the cross, then we don't have to carry them again in *our* bodies. Isaiah declared:

Yet it was our weaknesses he carried;
*   it was our sorrows that weighed him down.*
And we thought his troubles were a punishment from God,
*   a punishment for his own sins!*
But he was pierced for our rebellion,
*   crushed for our sins.*
He was beaten so we could be whole.
*   He was whipped so we could be healed.*
All of us, like sheep, have strayed away.
*   We have left God's paths to follow our own.*

> *Yet the* L*ORD* *laid on him*
> *the sins of us all.*
>
> Isaiah 53:4-6, NLT

But you cannot know and walk in the will of God until you are first transformed in your way of thinking:

> *Don't copy the behavior and customs of this world, but let God transform you into a new person by changing the way you think. Then you will learn to know God's will for you, which is good and pleasing and perfect.* Romans 12:2, NLT

Through divine judgment, we then command sickness and disease to get out in the name of Jesus Christ. This is called the authority of the saints.

The reason many don't get healed is because they are trying to earn it. They are thinking, "What do I need to do now that I have not done?" You don't need to do anything. Healing and miracles are already yours, paid for by Jesus Christ. All you must do is receive them by faith and rejoice in them.

Your healing is like a check. A check is money in disguise until you cash it or deposit it into your bank account. You can rejoice the moment you get it because you are now that much richer. You are blessed *"with all spiritual blessings,"* and that means you are not disadvantaged at all:

> *Blessed be the God and Father of our Lord Jesus Christ, who hath blessed us with all spiritual blessings in heavenly places in Christ.* Ephesians 1:3

There is a place in God prepared for you to excel and be free from sickness, disease, and failure. It is in Christ Jesus, and you are in Him now:

> *And these signs shall follow them that believe; In my name shall they cast out devils; they shall speak with new tongues; they shall take up serpents; and if they drink any deadly thing, it shall*

> *not hurt them; they shall lay hands on*
> *the sick, and they shall recover.* Mark
> 16:17-18

You cannot reign in life if you are trapped in failure and oppression. What Romans 5:17 says is true:

> *For if by one man's offence death reigned*
> *by one; much more they which receive*
> *abundance of grace and of the gift of*
> *righteousness shall reign in life by one,*
> *Jesus Christ.*

What Romans 8:1-2 says is real:

> *There is therefore now no condemnation*
> *to them which are in Christ Jesus, who*
> *walk not after the flesh, but after the*
> *Spirit. For the law of the Spirit of life*
> *in Christ Jesus hath made me free from*
> *the law of sin and death.*

Now, declare it and enforce it by faith:

All that the Father giveth me shall come to me; and him that cometh to me I will in no wise cast out.   John 6:37

And Joshua the son of Nun was full of the spirit of wisdom; for Moses had laid his hands upon him: and the children of Israel hearkened unto him, and did as the LORD commanded Moses.
                    Deuteronomy 34:9

You, too, can enjoy total freedom today. Why can you do all of this? Because you are now *In Charge!*

CHAPTER 3

FULLY IN CHARGE

Christ suffered for our sins once for all time. He never sinned, but he died for sinners to bring you safely home to God. He suffered physical death, but he was raised to life in the Spirit. 1 Peter 3:18, NLT

Rulership in the Kingdom of God is through the sacrifice of our Lord Jesus Christ. If you don't understand and believe that, you cannot rule. You are fully paid for, so that you can be fully in charge. You are fully backed by God to dominate or rule the Earth. Period!

What? know ye not that he which is joined to an harlot is one body? for two, saith he, shall be one flesh. But he that is joined unto the Lord is one spirit.

1 Corinthians 6:16-17

Through Christ we have an inheritance with God.

Furthermore, because we are united with Christ, we have received an inheritance from God, for he chose us in advance, and he makes everything work out according to his plan.

Ephesians 1:11, NLT

Part of our inheritance is ruling the Earth, because the Earth belonged to Him and *"the fullness thereof"* (Psalm 24:1). As long as Jesus is on the throne, our authority and dominion is intact. He is the Guarantor of our rulership:

Because of this oath, Jesus is the one who guarantees this better covenant with God. Hebrews 7:22, NLT

The surety of our covenant with God is not based on you or me, and it is not based on situations or circumstances. Christ is the surety that it has been done and done fully.

God said, *"I am the Lord who heals you"* (Exodus 15:26, NKJV). It's done! Moses declared, *"The LORD shall make you the head and not the tail"* (Deuteronomy 28:13, NKJV). It's done! Isaiah prophesied, *"No weapon formed against you shall prosper"* (Isaiah 54:17, NKJV). It's done! Paul wrote, *"My God shall supply all your need according to His riches in glory by Christ Jesus"* (Philippians 4:19, NKJV). It's done!

How can we be sure that all of these promises have been done? Because Jesus is the Surety. No wonder the Bible says, *"Looking unto Jesus the author and finisher of our faith"* (Hebrews 12:2).

Never ever doubt the Word of the living God. That's where you came from. The Word formed you. If you are a real human, then the Word is also real.

The penalty paid for the transgressions of humanity is the reason believers are now placed far above every other part of creation and given access to power, honor, blessing, wisdom, and riches:

> *And I beheld, and I heard the voice of many angels round about the throne and the beasts and the elders: and the number of them was ten thousand times ten thousand, and thousands of thousands; saying with a loud voice, Worthy is the Lamb that was slain to receive power, and riches, and wisdom, and strength, and honour, and glory, and blessing.* Revelation 5:11-12

You cannot be ridiculed anymore. You are in charge. You are an heir of God and a joint heir with Christ:

> *And if children, then heirs; heirs of God, and joint-heirs with Christ; if so be that we suffer with him, that we may be also glorified together.* Romans 8:17

> *Likewise, ye husbands, dwell with them*

> *according to knowledge, giving honour unto the wife, as unto the weaker vessel, and as being heirs together of the grace of life; that your prayers be not hindered.* 1 Peter 3:7

The coming of civilization, modernism, technology, science, and opinion has eroded the reality of the Truth written in the Holy Scriptures. The Babylonian system has taken over, and because some modern ideals don't honor the Word of God, they destroy the faith of many and bring them under bondage.

Many who quote the Scriptures never come to understand that it was the force behind Creation, the voice of the Lord God. That voice came to the prophets of old, and they saw the manifestation of what was spoken because God was in that voice.

No human voice could have stopped the movement of the sun and moon as happened in Joshua's time (see Joshua 10:12-13). That voice was later made flesh, and we saw the Word in Christ Jesus, our Lord:

> *And the Word was made flesh, and dwelt among us, (and we beheld his glory, the glory as of the only begotten of the Father,) full of grace and truth.*
>
> John 1:14

Now the voice of the Lord has been put into print, and we have it as the Bible. It is the same voice, just manifested in a different form.

When you understand why Jesus came to Earth, you will know why you must never suffer or be humiliated:

> *The thief cometh not, but for to steal, and to kill, and to destroy: I am come that they might have life, and that they might have it more abundantly.*
>
> John 10:10

> *He that committeth sin is of the devil; for the devil sinneth from the beginning. For this purpose the Son of God was manifested, that he might destroy the works of the devil.*   1 John 3:8

This is the revealed Word of God, and it is settled in Heaven, waiting for you to settle it in your own personal life by faith.

Christ is your substitute. He died to put you and me in charge. The position Jesus Christ occupied with the Father has been transferred to the Church through His blood:

> *Now ye are the body of Christ, and members in particular.*
>
> 1 Corinthians 12:27

This is why God won't do anything without your cooperation. When He sees you, He is seeing Christ in you. It is important for you to understand your righteous stand with God so that you can rule as He intended:

> *For he hath made him to be sin for us, who knew no sin; that we might be made the righteousness of God in him.*
>
> 2 Corinthians 5:21

> *For if by one man's offence death reigned*
> *by one; much more they which receive*
> *abundance of grace and of the gift of*
> *righteousness shall reign in life by one,*
> *Jesus Christ.* Romans 5:17

A sin-consciousness has been the reason people live in fear, anxiety, and doubt. They try their best to please God and earn His approval. Imagine how you would feel if you knew you had no fault at all, that you were pure and righteous and had access to the Father the way Jesus Christ had it. You would be able to change the world. Well, you are now righteous. The sad thing is that many don't yet know this and have not taken up their position of influence paid for by all that Jesus did and put into their account:

> *To wit, that God was in Christ, rec-*
> *onciling the world unto himself, not*
> *imputing their trespasses unto them;*
> *and hath committed unto us the word*
> *of reconciliation.* 2 Corinthians 5:19

God knew you couldn't be righteous on your own, that you couldn't pay for your righteous standing, so He gave you His righteousness as a gift. That is a license that puts you in the same class with Jesus. The goal is that every one of us should become like Christ.

You, my friend, are in the class of Elohim. You can call things that are not as though they were:

> *(As it is written, I have made thee a father of many nations,) before him whom he believed, even God, who quickeneth the dead, and calleth those things which be not as though they were.*
>
> Romans 4:17

It is the righteousness of Christ that gives us our placement and makes us righteous:

> *Confess your faults one to another, and pray one for another, that ye may be healed. The effectual fervent prayer of a righteous man availeth much.*   James 5:16

Now that we are righteous, anything can happen, so stop talking condemnation and intimidation. You have full access to the Father. The sin issue has been settled, and you can now shine:

> *Let us therefore come boldly unto the throne of grace, that we may obtain mercy, and find grace to help in time of need.* Hebrews 4:16

God laid the iniquities of us all upon Jesus long before we were born. That took care of past, present, and future. There is no sin to yet be committed that does not have a corresponding payment. You have been cleansed. All that God requires of us now is that we not go back and make a mockery of ourselves. You are clean; now don't go back to the mudhole of sin.

When Jesus met a woman caught in the act of adultery, it was a very bad situation. But look at what He said to her: *"Neither do I condemn you; go and sin no more"* (John 8:11). That settled her case.

THIS IS ONE OF THE MYSTERIES OF GOD'S KINGDOM

And he said, Unto you it is given to know the mysteries of the kingdom of God: but to others in parables; that seeing they might not see, and hearing they might not understand. Now the parable is this: The seed is the Word of God.

Luke 8:10-11

Your righteous stand transfers your battle to God on legal grounds. He is interested in fighting your cause and establishing you:

Behold, I have received commandment to bless: and he hath blessed; and I cannot reverse it. He hath not beheld iniquity in Jacob, neither hath he seen perverseness in Israel: the LORD his God is with him, and the shout of a king is among them. Numbers 23:20-21

The end of every affliction, frustration, premature death, and poverty is the shout of the King, Jesus Christ, the Son of God, who is with us. Therefore, we are good to go, and the enemy must now suffer devastation.

I am in charge. I am righteous in and through Christ Jesus and am exalted by my status in Him. It is this new status that puts me back in the Eden of God. This new Eden is spiritual, it is in Christ, and I am in Him, the Head of all principalities and powers:

For by him were all things created, that are in heaven, and that are in earth, visible and invisible, whether they be thrones, or dominions, or principalities, or powers: all things were created by him, and for him. Colossians 1:16

Whatever is not purified by the blood of Jesus cannot come in. Therefore we can challenge our challenges.

Jesus told a parable of a king who prepared a great party for his son. When the king went into the party, he noticed that there was a man without a wedding garment, and he called for the man to be punished:

> *So those servants went out into the highways, and gathered together all as many as they found, both bad and good: and the wedding was furnished with guests. And when the king came in to see the guests, he saw there a man which had not on a wedding garment: and he saith unto him, Friend, how camest thou in hither not having a wedding garment? And he was speechless.*
>
> *Then said the king to the servants, Bind him hand and foot, and take him away, and cast him into outer darkness, there shall be weeping and gnashing of teeth.*
>
> Matthew 22:10-13

In the same way, we have to say, "How did you get in here, sickness, diseases, cancer, oppression? You must go now. You are a thief and a robber. I cast you out now in Jesus' name, for I am in charge! Amen!" And our words will be obeyed.

We have the authority to pray like this:

1. Father, in the name of Jesus Christ, whatever is trying to come against my destiny that is not according to Your will and purpose, I command to cease now. Be removed! I reject your dominion over me in Jesus' name. *"For the rod of the wicked shall not rest upon the lot of the righteous"* (Psalm 125:3). In Jesus' name.

2. Father, in the name of Jesus Christ, because of my righteous stand with You, I decree now that favor, blessing, and breakthroughs begin to manifest in my life in Jesus Christ's name. Because I have received the gift of righteousness and I have abundance of grace, I am ruling now in Jesus' name.

3. Father, in the name of Jesus Christ, I shall never fail. *"The shout of the king"* is with me (Numbers 23:21). I therefore frustrate my frustrations, and I am free in Jesus' name.

4. Father, in the name of Jesus Christ, because I am in Eden now in and through Christ, premature death is not permitted here. Sickness is banished here. I am free and can do all things through Christ. No evil is permitted in this garden in the name of Jesus Christ.

5. Father, in the name of Jesus Christ, whatever the enemy or life's situation have brought into my life, I take out now. You are not permitted to be in my life. You have no permit, for you are not washed by the blood of Jesus. Get out now in His mighty name!

REDEMPTION REMOVED YOU COMPLETELY FROM THE DOMINION OF SIN AND DEATH

There is therefore now no condemnation to them which are in Christ Jesus, who walk not after the flesh, but after the Spirit. For the law of the Spirit of life in Christ Jesus hath made me free from the law of sin and death. Romans 8:1-2

Whatever the devil brings, you are exempt from it, for you have been given authority over everything that Jesus settled on Calvary. You stand before God with no guilt at all. He sees you as righteous and pure:

> *Yet now he has reconciled you to himself through the death of Christ in his physical body. As a result, he has brought you into his own presence, and you are holy and blameless as you stand before him without a single fault.*
>
> Colossians 1:22, NLT

This is true because you have changed governments and are no longer within Satan's jurisdiction:

> *For he has rescued us from the kingdom of darkness and transferred us into the Kingdom of his dear Son.*
>
> Colossians 1:13, NLT

The most wonderful part of it is that sin no longer has dominion over you:

For sin shall not have dominion over you: for ye are not under the law, but under grace. Romans 6:14

There is no law to break. It takes law for sin to hold you, and it takes breaking the law for you to be punished:

There is therefore now no condemnation to them which are in Christ Jesus, who walk not after the flesh, but after the Spirit. For the law of the Spirit of life in Christ Jesus hath made me free from the law of sin and death.
Romans 8:1-2

For Christ is the end of the law for righteousness to every one that believeth.
Romans 10:4

You now obey the Spirit of God through the Word of God:

But if ye be led of the Spirit, ye are not under the law. Galatians 5:18

"The mystery of godliness" is that God became man so that man can become god through the Word of God. He calls gods those to whom the Word has come:

> *The Holy Writings were given to them and God called them gods. (The Word of God cannot be put aside.)*
> John 10:35, NLT

When you speak now, it's not you the enemy is hearing. It's not you the situations and circumstances are hearing. It is God Himself:

> *Whoever listens to you, listens to Me. Whoever has nothing to do with you, has nothing to do with Me. Whoever has nothing to do with Me, has nothing to do with the One Who sent Me.*
> Luke 10:16, NLT

You are the echo of the Word. You are the Word manifest in the flesh. Why? Because you are joined with the Lord. You dare not speak against His Word, even when a situation looks dismal. Overcoming every situation is what makes you a god.

The covenant God cut with Abraham brought Jesus, and all the promises of God to Abraham were to be fulfilled in Christ. God told Abraham, *"Through your offspring all nations on earth will be blessed"* (Genesis 26:4). He was not referring only to Israel as a nation but to all the world that would come to God through Jesus and eventually become His legalized children:

> *Now the promise was made to Abraham and to his son. He does not say, "And to sons," speaking of many. But instead, "And to your Son," which means Christ.* Galatians 3:16, NLT

Israel is a nation that came through Abraham; the Church is a nation that comes to God through Christ. Under the covenant of God for the nation of Israel, God said:

> *By myself have I sworn, saith the LORD, for because thou hast done this thing,*

and hast not withheld thy son, thine only son: that in blessing I will bless thee, and in multiplying I will multiply thy seed as the stars of the heaven, and as the sand which is upon the sea shore; and thy seed shall possess the gate of his enemies; and in thy seed shall all the nations of the earth be blessed; because thou hast obeyed my voice.

Genesis 22:16-18

The covenant God cut with Jesus is more than just for the Church. He said:

Wherefore he is able also to save them to the uttermost that come unto God by him, seeing he ever liveth to make intercession for them.   Hebrews 7:25

There is therefore now no condemnation to them which are in Christ Jesus, who walk not after the flesh, but after the Spirit. ... In all these things we are more than conquerors through him that loved us.   Romans 8:1 and 37

For whatsoever is born of God overcometh the world: and this is the victory that overcometh the world, even our faith. Who is he that overcometh the world, but he that believeth that Jesus is the Son of God? 1 John 5:4-5

This is the reason you must know that you are a king placed here on Earth to rule.

What is our covenant? It is a divine agreement between God and man that is ratified by blood. Because blood is used as the seal, a life is involved. This is serious business, and anyone breaking the covenant will be cursed. God is forever faithful to His part of the covenant, and we must do ours.

In the primitive world, when a covenant was cut, it started with the exchange of gifts. Then the two parties cut themselves and shared each other's blood. It was a sacred moment.

God required the blood of Abraham in circumcision, and God gave Abraham His own blood through the ram that was caught in the thicket. Abraham knew, once this covenant was cut, that no one could stand against him in battle and win. His covenant friend, Yahweh, would destroy them:

> *And also that nation, whom they shall serve, will I judge: and afterward shall they come out with great substance. And thou shalt go to thy fathers in peace; thou shalt be buried in a good old age.*   Genesis 15:14-15

> *And I will establish my covenant between me and thee and thy seed after thee in their generations for an everlasting covenant, to be a God unto thee, and to thy seed after thee. And I will give unto thee, and to thy seed after thee, the land wherein thou art a stranger, all the land of Canaan, for an everlasting possession; and I will be their God.*   Genesis 17:7-8

That is what Jesus Christ did when He cut covenant with the Church. He said, *"This is my blood of the new testament [covenant]"*:

For this is my blood of the new testa-
ment, which is shed for many for the
remission of sins. Matthew 26:28

In that moment, sin was pardoned and was gone, as if had never been committed.

When you understand covenant, you will know why it is impossible not to rule and why your faith must go to another level. It is that covenant that legalizes you to use the name of Jesus Christ and get results. God backs the use of that name because of the covenant, and God has never changed.

The covenant of God with the Church brought the Holy Spirit here. This terminated every curse and initiated the promises of God:

Christ hath redeemed us from the curse
of the law, being made a curse for us: for
it is written, Cursed is every one that
hangeth on a tree: that the blessing of
Abraham might come on the Gentiles
through Jesus Christ; that we might
receive the promise of the Spirit through
faith. Galatians 3:13-14

We received the promise of the Spirit through faith, and *"where the Spirit of the Lord is, there is liberty"* (2 Corinthians 3:17).

There can be no intimidation when the Holy Spirit is with you and residing in you:

> *And I will restore to you the years that the locust hath eaten, the cankerworm, and the caterpiller, and the palmerworm, my great army which I sent among you. And ye shall eat in plenty, and be satisfied, and praise the name of the LORD your God, that hath dealt wondrously with you: and my people shall never be ashamed. And ye shall know that I am in the midst of Israel, and that I am the LORD your God, and none else: and my people shall never be ashamed.*
>
> *And it shall come to pass afterward, that I will pour out my spirit upon all flesh; and your sons and your daughters shall prophesy, your old men shall dream dreams, your young men shall see visions.*   Joel 2:25-28

Satan cannot bind you when you have the Holy Ghost in you—never. Jesus promised to send the Spirit, and He fulfilled that in the book of Acts. Now the Spirit of God lives in you and abides in you forever.

When Abraham cut covenant with God, he was a nobody, but God changed his story. He was poor and barren, but God made him a nation and defended him. In the time of famine, God sustained him so that he never felt lack. His life was now God's responsibility.

That covenant affected Isaac, Abraham's son. In a time of famine, he actually progressed and excelled:

> *Then Isaac sowed in that land, and received in the same year an hundredfold: and the LORD blessed him. And the man waxed great, and went forward, and grew until he became very great: for he had possession of flocks, and possession of herds, and great store of servants: and the Philistines envied him.*
>
> Genesis 26:12-14

As a result of the covenant, the plague that devastated Egypt never came close to the houses of God's children. The covenant sustained them in famine and in war. God stood up for them, and they didn't have to do anything except believe in the covenant and obeyed God's instructions. The rest was up to God.

When they left Egypt and returned to possess the Promised Land, God told them to march around the walls of the armed city of Jericho. The only other thing they needed to do to possess it was shout. Such a military strategy had never been recorded, but that was God's strategy.

The covenant brought Jesus Christ, and you must know that no diseases will be allowed to come near your dwelling place. Why? Because of the covenant.

> *Have respect unto the covenant: for the dark places of the earth are full of the habitations of cruelty.*   Psalm 74:20

The cruelty of darkness can't come near God's beloved children. God went so far as to be incarnate in a woman's womb to make sure the covenant was properly established. Jesus was not the son of Joseph, nor of Abraham, nor of David. He was God in human flesh:

> *Jesus said unto them, Verily, verily, I say unto you, Before Abraham was, I am.* John 8:58

> *What think ye of Christ? whose son is he? They say unto him, The son of David. He saith unto them, How then doth David in spirit call him Lord, saying, the Lord said unto my Lord, Sit thou on my right hand, till I make thine enemies thy footstool? If David then call him Lord, how is he his son?* Matthew 22:42-45

You and I are the ministers of the new covenant, *"not of the letter but of the spirit: for the letter killeth but spirit giveth life"* (2 Corinthians 3:6).

Get this right: God created the heavens and the earth with the intention of man ruling over it and dominating it. Man "messed up" and gave it to the devil. But then God stepped in and restored man to his place of rulership:

> *And to Seth, to him also there was born*
> *a son; and he called his name Enos: then*
> *began men to call upon the name of the*
> *LORD.* Genesis 4:26

With Enos, man returned to and begin serving God once again. Things went along fine then ... until a group of proud men began building a tower to Heaven, a government without God. God had to send confusion into their midst. Then God looked for a priest who would represent Him on Earth. He found Abraham and cut covenant with Him.

Abraham then ruled and dominated the Earth, and God promised that his descendants would be priest unto Him:

> *And ye shall be unto me a kingdom of*
> *priests, and an holy nation. These are*

*the words which thou shalt speak unto
the children of Israel.*   Exodus 19:6

The entire nation of Israel was to serve as God's representatives on Earth. However, they, too, "messed up" and followed and worshipped idols. These abominations repelled God, and He decided to choose one tribe from among them to stand out and bring the people back to Him. The members of this tribe were descendants of Levi and were known as Levites.

In time, even the Levites compromised, and God had to look to Himself to raise up a priest to honor Him, and He found Jesus, of the house and tribe of God:

> *But Christ as a son over his own house;
> whose house are we, if we hold fast the
> confidence and the rejoicing of the hope
> firm unto the end.*   Hebrews 3:6

God had to turn inward, to His own Son, to do His bidding and rule the Earth.

When Jesus had finished His job, and was looking for a family who would be priests unto God and take over the Earth, He found the Church and called it His Body. You and I are now called the priests of the Most High God:

> *But ye are a chosen generation, a royal priesthood, an holy nation, a peculiar people; that ye should shew forth the praises of him who hath called you out of darkness into his marvellous light.*
>
> 1 Peter 2:9

God had foretold through Joel:

> *And ye shall eat in plenty, and be satisfied, and praise the name of the LORD your God, that hath dealt wondrously with you: and my people shall never be ashamed. And ye shall know that I am in the midst of Israel, and that I am the LORD your God, and none else: and my people shall never be ashamed.*
>
> *And it shall come to pass afterward, that*

I will pour out my spirit upon all flesh; and your sons and your daughters shall prophesy, your old men shall dream dreams, your young men shall see visions. Joel 2:26-28

There is something special in and on you now. It is the power of the Holy Spirit. You are a priest of the Most High, so you cannot fail. This is called the election of grace:

I will also clothe her priests with salvation: and her saints shall shout aloud for joy. Psalm 132:16

But ye shall be named the Priests of the LORD: men shall call you the Ministers of our God: ye shall eat the riches of the Gentiles, and in their glory shall ye boast yourselves. Isaiah 61:6

It's time to declare victory, time to triumph over every enemy. No evil is permitted here in God's Kingdom. No counsel of the enemy shall rule you in the name of Jesus Christ.

Take your God-given authority and make declarations like these:

1. Father, in the name of Jesus Christ, I praise You that I am not under the Law. The law of sin and death cannot hold me bound. I declare my liberty and freedom now. Satan, you cannot touch me in Jesus' name.

2. Father, in the name of Jesus, he that hears me hears you. Hear the word of the Lord now. Favor come to me now, along with joy and peace. I stop you now, cancer, diabetes, and pain. Failure, go, and never come back here again in the name of Jesus Christ.

3. Father, in the name of Jesus Christ, I am in covenant with Yahweh, the God of Abraham, Isaac, and Jacob, and our covenant forbids failure, stagnation, and frustration. I command them to stop now in Jesus' name.

4. Father, in the name of Jesus, by the covenant of God upon me, I have joy, peace,

prosperity, and longevity. Through the power in the blood of Jesus, I am in charge now in Jesus' name.

5. Father, in the name of Jesus Christ, I escape every wickedness of the enemy today. You have respect for the covenant, and I declare by the power of the covenant that enough is enough in the name of Jesus Christ. Enough, affliction! Enough, sickness! Enough, lack! My heavens are open, and I am taking charge now. Evil, get out of my territory now in the name of Jesus Christ.

Remember Jehovah Elohim made the Heaven and Earth, and He made other Elohim that joined Him in the administration of the Universe.

Genesis 1:26 shows that God was talking to some beings that were in that administration. That was His way of operation.

Psalm 82:1-2 makes us to know that there are beings that are created as Elohim but are not Yahweh. So, after the rebellion of Lucifer, these Elohim became gods that wanted attention for themselves and wanted the rulership of the Universe to be through them. When man fell, they seduced him to follow and worship them rather than God:

> *Hath any of the gods of the nations delivered at all his land out of the hand of the king of Assyria? Where are the gods of Hamath, and of Arpad? where are the gods of Sepharvaim, Hena, and Ivah? have they delivered Samaria out of mine hand? Who are they among all the gods of the countries, that have delivered their country out of mine hand, that the LORD should deliver Jerusalem out of mine hand?*
>
> 2 Kings 18:33-35

This was the Syrian commander ranting about his gods. When God warned Israel in the Ten Commandments, *"Thou shall have no other god before me,"* He was talking about the gods of the Earth:

*And God spake all these words, saying, I am the L*ORD *thy God, which have brought thee out of the land of Egypt, out of the house of bondage. Thou shalt have no other gods before me.*

Exodus 20:1-3

Paul said

For though there be that are called gods, whether in heaven or in earth, (as there be gods many, and lords many,) but to us there is but one God, the Father, of whom are all things, and we in him; and one Lord Jesus Christ, by whom are all things, and we by him. 1 Corinthians 8:5-6

These gods fraternized with humans, deceived them, and then lured them into rebellion against Yahweh, the one true God. That was why God disinherited the Earth and decided to form a family for Himself among mankind.

The real God, Yahweh, met with Abraham and cut covenant with him. The intention was to raise a family again on the Earth so that the garden of Eden experience could continue:

And when Abram was ninety years old and nine, the LORD appeared to Abram, and said unto him, I am the Almighty God; walk before me, and be thou perfect. And I will make my covenant between me and thee, and will multiply thee exceedingly.

And Abram fell on his face: and God talked with him, saying, as for me, behold, my covenant is with thee, and thou shalt be a father of many nations. Neither shall thy name any more be called Abram, but thy name shall be Abraham; for a father of many nations have I made thee. And I will make thee exceeding fruitful, and I will make nations of thee, and kings shall come out of thee. And I will establish my covenant between me and thee and thy seed after thee in their generations for an everlasting covenant, to be a God unto thee, and to thy seed after thee. Genesis 17:1-7

God wanted to work through this man. He wanted to use his descendants to shame the gods other nations were serving. He wanted them to know that serving Him would bring them many benefits and authority over the Earth realm. After all, it belonged to Him:

> *And ye shall serve the LORD your God, and he shall bless thy bread, and thy water; and I will take sickness away from the midst of thee. There shall nothing cast their young, nor be barren, in thy land: the number of thy days I will fulfil.*　　　Exodus 23:25-26

God told Israel, "I am the one who delivered you out of Egypt from the hands of other gods and lords." It was not just the firstborn of the Egyptians that God destroyed; He also destroyed the gods of Egypt:

> *For I will pass through the land of Egypt this night, and will smite all the firstborn in the land of Egypt, both man and*

> *beast; and against all the gods of Egypt*
> *I will execute judgment: I am the* Lord.
> Exodus 12:12

These other gods and their forces contested with the children of God by manipulating them through their senses and their environment, that is until Jesus Christ, God in human form, came:

> *In the beginning was the Word, and the Word was with God, and the Word was God. The same was in the beginning with God. All things were made by him; and without him was not any thing made that was made.* John 1:1-3

Again, Jesus was not the son of Joseph; He was and is God Himself. He did take the form of a man, but He did it to put man back in charge of running the Universe:

> *But as many as received him, to them gave he power to become the sons of God, even to them that believe on his name:*

> *which were born, not of blood, nor of the*
> *will of the flesh, nor of the will of man,*
> *but of God.*   John 1:12-13

It was the inability of man to rule the Earth without disturbance that caused Jesus to come here. Again, *"the mystery of godliness"* is that God became man so that man could become a god through the Word of God:

> *And without controversy great is the*
> *mystery of godliness: God was manifest*
> *in the flesh, justified in the Spirit, seen*
> *of angels, preached unto the Gentiles,*
> *believed on in the world, received up*
> *into glory.*   1 Timothy 3:16

> *To whom God would make known what*
> *is the riches of the glory of this mystery*
> *among the Gentiles; which is Christ in*
> *you, the hope of glory.* Colossians 1:27

Unfortunately many people don't see this. Why? Paul wrote:

> *In whom the god of this world hath blinded the minds of them which believe not, lest the light of the glorious gospel of Christ, who is the image of God, should shine unto them.*
>
> 2 Corinthians 4:4

People are so blind that they wrestle against truth. Their human philosophies are almost always against what God is saying. They limit us when God said we could *"do all things through Christ"* (Philippians 4:13). They limit us when God said He would *"supply all [my] need according to his riches in glory by Christ Jesus"* (Philippians 4:19).

I have adoption papers ratified by the blood of Jesus that declare me to be the legal heir:

> *But when the fulness of the time was come, God sent forth his Son, made of a woman, made under the law.* Galatians 4:4

> *And hast made us unto our God kings and priests: and we shall reign on the earth.* Revelation 5:10

Jesus' coming was to put a total end to the reign of darkness and reinstall man in His original position. Even though Jesus did this, many still act like slaves. He said:

Behold, I give unto you power to tread on serpents and scorpions, and over all the power of the enemy: and nothing shall by any means hurt you. Luke 10:19

John, writing to the early Church, said, *"I have written unto you ... because ye have known him that is from the beginning. I have written unto you ... because ye are strong, and the word of God abideth in you, and ye have overcome the wicked one"* (1 John 2:14). He also declared:

We know that whosoever is born of God sinneth not; but he that is begotten of God keepeth himself, and that wicked one toucheth him not. 1 John 5:18

The Word makes you a god, one of the Elohim:

> *If he called them gods, unto whom the Word of God came, and the scripture cannot be broken; say ye of him, whom the Father hath sanctified, and sent into the world, Thou blasphemest; because I said, I am the Son of God? If I do not the works of my Father, believe me not. But if I do, though ye believe not me, believe the works: that ye may know, and believe, that the Father is in me, and I in him.* John 10:35-38

God's Word is the description of what He wants you to become in His world. We are so used to the world we live in that we no longer see it as being God's world. The life Jesus lived here was not in the world as we know it, but in God's world. Nothing was missing, and nothing was broken, and He called things into being by the authority of the Father. We, too, are invited to this world through believing and obeying the Scriptures.

The whole world has been deceived so that men no longer see this world as God's government that rules the world of men:

Then said Jesus to them again, Peace be
unto you: as my Father hath sent me,
even so send I you.   John 20:21

The foundation for ruling on Earth is the
Word of God and your perfect positioning
in Christ. No matter what, the Word always
prevails:

Even if everyone else is a liar, God is
true. As the Scriptures say about him,
"You will be proved right in what you say,
*   and you will win your case in*
court."   Romans 3:4, NLT

Every time faith is released in the Word of God,
you are in charge. In Abraham's day, everything
obeyed him because he lived in God's world and
believed and obeyed the Word of God:

For the promise, that he should be the
heir of the world, was not to Abraham,
or to his seed, through the law, but
through the righteousness of faith.
                    Romans 4:13

You start ruling when you start believing in God's world, which is the Spirit realm explained and displayed by and through the Word of God. That which is invisible is clearly seen by the spoken and written Word of God.

Here's what God's Book says about me and you:

> *You made all the delicate, inner parts of my body*
> *and knit me together in my mother's womb.*
> *Thank you for making me so wonderfully complex!*
> *Your workmanship is marvelous—how well I know it.*
> *You watched me as I was being formed in utter seclusion,*
> *as I was woven together in the dark of the womb.*
> *You saw me before I was born.*
> *Every day of my life was recorded in your book.*

Every moment was laid out
before a single day had passed.
Psalm 139:13-16, NLT

God already said that His thoughts toward me are for peace and not evil, and now I see that all my days are written in the Book. What the devil does is to sow tares and confusion, but God already wrote the book about you and me and sealed it. If there are things not written that you see, then let your Advocate know about it. He always wins in court. Now declare with authority:

1. Father, in the name of Jesus Christ, every god ruling any area of my life and destiny, must stop right now. False gods, I stop your operation in Jesus' name.

2. Father, in the name of Jesus Christ, I am adopted legally into the family of Yahweh. Therefore, nothing will ever stop me from shining again. I am fully in charge in Jesus' name.

3. Father, in the name of Jesus Christ, the Book written about me does not include sickness, diseases, poverty, affliction, or failure. Therefore I command these to leave me now.

We are not only created in the image of God; we are designed to function like Him as a god on Earth:

> *And God said, Let us make man in our image, after our likeness: and let them have dominion over the fish of the sea, and over the fowl of the air, and over the cattle, and over all the earth, and over every creeping thing that creepeth upon the earth.* Genesis 1:26

God functions only by faith, so faith is a requirement for us in order to take charge of things:

> *Through faith we understand that the worlds were framed by the word of God, so that things which are seen were not*

made of things which do appear. ...
But without faith it is impossible to
please him: for he that cometh to God
must believe that he is, and that he is
a rewarder of them that diligently seek
him.   Hebrews 11:3 and 6

God's Word declares, *"The just shall live by faith"* (Romans i:17). Faith is a living force that engages the living Word so that we can live a victorious life:

For whatsoever is born of God overco-
meth the world: and this is the victory
that overcometh the world, even our
faith.   1 John 5:4

Faith is not real until the evidence of it is visible. If you have physical proof, you are not using faith. You just have made mental ascent to it. You don't have to see faith or feel it, but you believe something because God said it, and therefore you begin speaking it:

> *We having the same spirit of faith, according as it is written, I believed, and therefore have I spoken; we also believe, and therefore speak.*
>
> 2 Corinthians 4:13

God's faith is a speaking faith. He trusts Himself and His word to the extent that when He speaks, He knows that what He has spoken is done. Therefore, He *"calls those things which be not as though they were"*:

> *(As it is written, I have made thee a father of many nations,) before him whom he believed, even God, who quickeneth the dead, and calleth those things which be not as though they were.*
>
> Romans 4:17

> *And Jesus answering saith unto them, Have faith in God. For verily I say unto you, That whosoever shall say unto this mountain, Be thou removed, and be thou cast into the sea; and shall not doubt in his heart, but shall believe that those*

*things which he saith shall come to pass;
he shall have whatsoever he saith.*

Mark 11:22-23

*Who being the brightness of his glory,
and the express image of his person,
and upholding all things by the word
of his power, when he had by himself
purged our sins, sat down on the right
hand of the Majesty on high.*

Hebrews 1:3

The Word keeps what faith has purchased. It doesn't matter who is occupying your property, you have the title deed, and any interlopers will soon have to vacate the premises:

*Now faith is the assurance (the confirmation, the title deed) of the things [we]
hope for, being the proof of things [we]
do not see and the conviction of their
reality [faith perceiving as real fact what
is not revealed to the senses].*

Hebrews 11:1, AMPC

That is why God said through Joel, *"I will restore":*

> *And I will restore to you the years that the locust hath eaten, the cankerworm, and the caterpiller, and the palmerworm, my great army which I sent among you.* Joel 2:25

When God says, "I will restore," faith says, "Yes, Sir." How will He do it? That's none of our business. The important thing is that everything is coming back to us, plus a bonus. Stir up the supernatural by speaking the Word of faith, which is right there in your mouth.

When God said through Elisha, "By this time tomorrow there shall be plenty at the gate of Samaria, and it will be cheap," faith said, "Okay, thank You!" Those who said, "That's impossible," died:

> *Then Elisha said, Hear ye the word of the LORD; Thus saith the LORD, To*

morrow about this time shall a measure of fine flour be sold for a shekel, and two measures of barley for a shekel, in the gate of Samaria. Then a lord on whose hand the king leaned answered the man of God, and said, Behold, if the LORD would make windows in heaven, might this thing be? And he said, Behold, thou shalt see it with thine eyes, but shalt not eat thereof. 2 Kings 7:1-2

Salvation does not come by feeling but by speaking:

For with the heart man believeth unto righteousness; and with the mouth confession is made unto salvation.
Romans 10:10

Health can come the same way, as can prosperity and breakthrough. When anything and everything tries to pull us back into the natural, we must not agree with it. Otherwise we will lose control over the Earth:

> *But the natural man receiveth not the*
> *things of the Spirit of God: for they are*
> *foolishness unto him: neither can he know*
> *them, because they are spiritually dis-*
> *cerned. But he that is spiritual judgeth all*
> *things, yet he himself is judged of no man.*
> *For who hath known the mind of the Lord,*
> *that he may instruct him? but we have the*
> *mind of Christ.* 1 Corinthians 2:14-16

The great majority of Christian believers "mess up" God's plan because they center their attention on who they were before they met Christ and not on what and who they are now in Him. When the attention is not on who we are in Christ, we lose our supernatural reputation:

> *If ye then be risen with Christ, seek those*
> *things which are above, where Christ*
> *sitteth on the right hand of God.*
>   Colossians 3:1

When Jesus rose from the dead, He stood before the Father as the firstborn of every creation, and He is the Advocate for the Church. Once we are born again, He will never leave us unprotected. We are in Him, and that is now our Eden:

> *For ye are dead, and your life is hid with Christ in God.*   Colossians 3:3

Whatever we do is now acceptable in the court room of Heaven through Christ, our Advocate. In Him, we are complete. In Him, we are favored. In Him, we are healed. In Him, we are more than conquerors. Our rulership on Earth is only guaranteed in Him. Being in Him makes us a legal resident of the Kingdom, and we need not be bothered about anything. In Him, is the fullness of God:

> *For in him dwelleth all the fulness of the Godhead bodily. And ye are complete in him, which is the head of all principality and power.*   Colossians 2:9-10

Because you and I are in Christ, even though we live on Earth physically, we are enjoying the benefits of Heaven. Please see the truth of God's Word, believe it, and act on it:

> *And hath raised us up together, and made us sit together in heavenly places in Christ Jesus.*   Ephesians 2:6

This takes off the limits from our position and authority. We are already seated with Him:

> *The like figure whereunto even baptism doth also now save us (not the putting away of the filth of the flesh, but the answer of a good conscience toward God,) by the resurrection of Jesus Christ: who is gone into heaven, and is on the right hand of God; angels and authorities and powers being made subject unto him.*
>   1 Peter 3:21-22

Since we are in Christ, that makes us untouchable for Satan and his host of darkness. This lets me know what is going on in Heaven now through the Holy Spirit:

For in him we live, and move, and have our being; as certain also of your own poets have said, For we are also his off-spring. Acts 17:28

Meditate on this, and then act on it:

For though there be that are called gods, whether in heaven or in earth, (as there be gods many, and lords many,) but to us there is but one God, the Father, of whom are all things, and we in him; and one Lord Jesus Christ, by whom are all things, and we by him. 1 Corinthians 8:5-6

For this is as the waters of Noah unto me: for as I have sworn that the waters of Noah should no more go over the earth; so have I sworn that I would not be wroth with thee, nor rebuke thee. For the mountains shall depart, and the hills be removed; but my kindness shall not depart from thee, neither shall the covenant of my peace be removed, saith the LORD *that hath mercy on thee.* Isaiah 54:9-10

The Place of Financial Stability in Rulership

Without financial stability and strength you will never be in charge on Earth. *"Money answers all things"* (Ecclesiastes 10:19, NKJV).

> *Wealth maketh many friends; but the poor is separated from his neighbour.*
> Proverbs 19:4

> *The poor man's wisdom is despised.*
> Ecclesiastes 9:16, NKJV

When you have financial freedom, captivity is overturned.

Financial hardship is a curse. It is one of the ways God shows His disagreement and anger over our disobedience. It came about in the first place as a result of disobedience to God's Word:

> *And unto Adam he said, Because thou hast hearkened unto the voice of thy*

156

wife, and hast eaten of the tree, of which I commanded thee, saying, Thou shalt not eat of it: cursed is the ground for thy sake; in sorrow shalt thou eat of it all the days of thy life; thorns also and thistles shall it bring forth to thee; and thou shalt eat the herb of the field; in the sweat of thy face shalt thou eat bread, till thou return unto the ground; for out of it wast thou taken: for dust thou art, and unto dust shalt thou return.

Genesis 3:17-19

If redemption is to be complete, then it must include the restoration of wealth and blessing. Never forget what happened the moment man was put into the garden. Genesis 1:28 says, *"And God blessed them."* He is still blessing those of us who are in Christ:

Unto you first God, having raised up his Son Jesus, sent him to bless you, in turning away every one of you from his iniquities. Acts 3:26

You are saved to be blessed. The power of the curse is gone completely through your redemption in Christ:

> *Christ hath redeemed us from the curse of the law, being made a curse for us: for it is written, Cursed is every one that hangeth on a tree: that the blessing of Abraham might come on the Gentiles through Jesus Christ; that we might receive the promise of the Spirit through faith.* Galatians 3:13-14

When Jesus came, He swallowed up poverty completely:

> *For ye know the grace of our Lord Jesus Christ, that, though he was rich, yet for your sakes he became poor, that ye through his poverty might be rich.*
> 2 Corinthians 8:9

Every child of God must know that to be poor is not godly, and it is also not humility. Being poor is, in fact, robbery:

Let them shout for joy, and be glad, that favour my righteous cause: yea, let them say continually, Let the LORD *be magnified, which hath pleasure in the prosperity of his servant.* Psalm 35:27

God takes pleasure in the prosperity of His servants. In other words, your connection to God as the Source of your life puts you above financial reproach. The world system, the Babylonian system, introduced poverty. There is no poverty at all in God's Kingdom. Poverty is a deviation from God's norm:

But thou shalt remember the LORD *thy God: for it is he that giveth thee power to get wealth, that he may establish his covenant which he sware unto thy fathers, as it is this day.*
Deuteronomy 8:18

God has a plan for His covenant children and has given us power to gain wealth. You can't handle this power and not know that it's real. This it not trial and error. It's

real, and it will work for you—if you apply
yourself.

It takes wisdom, not methods, to amass
wealth. The whole world is looking for
strange manifestations of God in our lives,
and as they see them, they will bow to the
Lordship of Jesus Christ:

> *And when the sabbath day was come,
> he began to teach in the synagogue:
> and many hearing him were aston-
> ished, saying, From whence hath this
> man these things? and what wisdom is
> this which is given unto him, that even
> such mighty works are wrought by his
> hands?* Mark 6:2

God doesn't have favorites. He is not a
respecter of persons:

> *Then Peter opened his mouth, and said, Of
> a truth I perceive that God is no respecter
> of persons: but in every nation he that
> feareth him, and worketh righteousness, is
> accepted with him.* Acts 10:34-35

Many know what the Bible says, but relatively few are willing to apply themselves to its demands.

Every Kingdom provision is packaged in secrets. When you lay hold of those secrets, you can master your world. This is not a gimmick. The devil has perverted the truth and sold lies to the masses. God has given us the truth of His Word.

Kingdom wealth is not just being able to eat, drink, and be comfortable until you die. No, Kingdom wealth is also about being able to bless others out of your fullness:

> *And the LORD shall make thee plenteous in goods, in the fruit of thy body, and in the fruit of thy cattle, and in the fruit of thy ground, in the land which the LORD sware unto thy fathers to give thee.*
> Deuteronomy 28:11

You cannot feed the poor and clothe the naked if you don't have enough yourself, and you are commissioned to do just that:

Then shall the King say unto them on his right hand, Come, ye blessed of my Father, inherit the kingdom prepared for you from the foundation of the world: for I was an hungred, and ye gave me meat: I was thirsty, and ye gave me drink: I was a stranger, and ye took me in: naked, and ye clothed me: I was sick, and ye visited me: I was in prison, and ye came unto me.

Then shall the righteous answer him, saying, Lord, when saw we thee an hungred, and fed thee? or thirsty, and gave thee drink? When saw we thee a stranger, and took thee in? or naked, and clothed thee? Or when saw we thee sick, or in prison, and came unto thee? And the King shall answer and say unto them, Verily I say unto you, Inasmuch as ye have done it unto one of the least of these my brethren, ye have done it unto me.   Matthew 25:34-40

Kingdom wealth has nothing to do with your profession or career. It's all about understanding the secrets of God and your willingness to obey His commands. You might be a teacher, a doctor, a coach, an accountant, or any number of other positions in modern society. It makes no difference. Kingdom wealth works for anyone:

> *For whom he did foreknow, he also did predestinate to be conformed to the image of his Son, that he might be the firstborn among many brethren. Moreover whom he did predestinate, them he also called: and whom he called, them he also justified: and whom he justified, them he also glorified.*
>
> Romans 8:29-30

All you need is a good understanding, and you can quickly enter into irreversible wealth and abundance:

> *Good understanding giveth favour: but the way of transgressors is hard.*
>
> Proverbs 13:15

If you can take hold of these secrets today, you can become, not only a wealthy person, but also a distributor of wealth. This will work because these truths are based on God's Word, not someone's opinion.

Here are some keys to your prosperity:

1. **Obedience:** You will never produce wealth until you recognize the true Source of wealth and learn to obey. That Source is not your job or your business. It's God. He may use your business to connect you with great opportunities, but He is the Source.

The Word of God and obedience to that Word is the key to anything and everything on Earth. Never forget: it was disobedience that brought poverty. God told Adam and Eve not to eat of the forbidden fruit. However, because they found that this fruit was *"pleasant to the eyes"* (Genesis 3:6), they bowed to its lure and lost everything:

> *If they obey and serve him, they shall spend their days in prosperity, and their years in pleasures.*   Job 36:11

That's a big *IF*.

The Spirit of God is always present to direct us, if we are committed to His instructions. If not, we will miss the blessing.

To sow in a time of famine seems absurd, but that's just what Isaac did, and he reaped a hundredfold return (see Genesis 26:12). Obedience to the Word of God, regardless of the circumstances, brings blessing.

In John 2:5, Mary, the mother of Jesus, said, *"Whatsoever he saith unto you, do it."* You cannot choose when to obey and when not to obey. Every harvest has a season, and if you miss your season, you will have to stand in line for the next one. Obey when the Spirit speaks.

2. **Giving:** The Kingdom way of prospering its citizens is completely different from the way of the world:

> *While the earth remaineth, seedtime and harvest, and cold and heat, and summer and winter, and day and night shall not cease.* Genesis 8:22

If you are not a sower, you will end up a beggar, for everything was created in seed form. God gives the seed, and you do the planting. If you don't plant the seed, you will never reap your harvest.

Naming your seed is not God's duty either; it's yours. God will bring the seed to you, but you must name the harvest it will produce and do it according to His will.

Many eat their seed rather than be obedient to the Word of God. We are to sow as God directs us. You don't just give. There are specific ways to give that bring a guaranteed blessing.

Give Tithes

Financial freedom begins with tithing. If you fail to tithe, you will never escape a closed Heaven. Today we don't tithe as a law; we do it as a covenant obligation. The Law of Moses did not yet exist when God taught Abraham the blessing of tithing, and this man went on to become the possessor of Heaven and Earth:

And Melchizedek king of Salem brought forth bread and wine: and he was the priest of the most high God. And he blessed him, and said, Blessed be Abram of the most high God, possessor of heaven and earth: and blessed be the most high God, which hath delivered thine enemies into thy hand. And he gave him tithes of all. Genesis 14:18-20

The Law came so that we could appreciate the power of the covenant. God said, *"Prove me ... if I will not open the windows of heaven and pour you out a blessing"* (Malachi 3:10). The New Living Translation of the Bible renders that verse like this:

"Bring all the tithes into the storehouse so there will be enough food in my Temple. If you do," says the LORD of Heaven's Armies, "I will open the windows of heaven for you. I will pour out a blessing so great you won't have enough room to take it in! Try it! Put me to the test!"

You are not enriching God when you tithe; you are opening financial destiny for yourself:

> *And all the tithe of the land, whether of the seed of the land, or of the fruit of the tree, is the LORD's: it is holy unto the LORD. ...*
>
> *And concerning the tithe of the herd, or of the flock, even of whatsoever passeth under the rod, the tenth shall be holy unto the LORD.*　Leviticus 27:30 and 32

Tithing provokes Heaven's intervention. God said, *"I will rebuke the devourer for your sake"* (Malachi 3:11). This follows Malachi's teaching on tithing"

> *Will a man rob God? Yet ye have robbed me. But ye say, Wherein have we robbed thee? In tithes and offerings. Ye are cursed with a curse: for ye have robbed me, even this whole nation. Bring ye all the tithes into the storehouse, that there may be meat in mine house, and prove*

me now herewith, saith the LORD of hosts, if I will not open you the windows of heaven, and pour you out a blessing, that there shall not be room enough to receive it. Malachi 3:8-10

Jesus taught against the Pharisees' abuses of tithing:

But woe unto you, Pharisees! for ye tithe mint and rue and all manner of herbs, and pass over judgment and the love of God: these ought ye to have done, and not to leave the other undone. Luke 11:42

The tithe is not the same as a freewill offering. The tithe is God's portion that you keep for Him. He knows the amount of it, so don't be guilty of stealing from it or diverting it to other uses.

Give Offerings

An offering is what you bring to the altar as an appreciation for who God is to you:

Therefore if thou bring thy gift to the altar, and there rememberest that thy brother hath ought against thee; leave there thy gift before the altar, and go thy way; first be reconciled to thy brother, and then come and offer thy gift.

Matthew 5:23

Upon the first day of the week let every one of you lay by him in store, as God hath prospered him, that there be no gatherings when I come.

1 Corinthians 16:2

Three times in a year shall all thy males appear before the LORD *thy God in the place which he shall choose; in the feast of unleavened bread, and in the feast of weeks, and in the feast of tabernacles: and they shall not appear before the* LORD *empty: every man shall give as he is able, according to the blessing of the* LORD *thy God which he hath given thee.*

Deuteronomy 16:16-17

We are commanded not to appear empty before the Lord. If you don't have money to offer, sow your time, your love, your commitment and dedication. But never appear empty before the King, for this is an insult to Him.

Are you expecting fire to fall from Heaven? Well, fire never falls on an empty altar. There must be a sacrifice placed there.

Give Kingdom Advancement Gifts

This means God is asking us to give because there is a need in His house and He wants us to be part of the answer. This, again, is an act of sacrifice. Every Kingdom project is for our progress, so every time a project is announced in your church, get excited and do your part:

> *And Moses spake unto all the congregation of the children of Israel, saying, This is the thing which the Lord commanded, saying, Take ye from among you an offering unto the Lord:*

whosoever is of a willing heart, let him bring it, an offering of the LORD; gold, and silver, and brass.   Exodus 35:4-5

For thus saith the LORD of hosts; Yet once, it is a little while, and I will shake the heavens, and the earth, and the sea, and the dry land; and I will shake all nations, and the desire of all nations shall come: and I will fill this house with glory, saith the LORD of hosts. The silver is mine, and the gold is mine, saith the LORD of hosts.   Haggai 2:6-8

And this gospel of the kingdom shall be preached in all the world for a witness unto all nations; and then shall the end come.   Matthew 24:14

If you want to be part of the spread of the Gospel in Jesus' name, this kind of giving brings manifold returns.

And Jesus answered and said, Verily I say unto you, There is no man that hath left house, or brethren, or sisters, or father, or mother, or wife, or children, or lands, for my sake, and the gospel's, but he shall receive an hundredfold now in this time, houses, and brethren, and sisters, and mothers, and children, and lands, with persecutions; and in the world to come eternal life.

Mark 10:29-30

Give To the Prophets

Giving to the prophets opens a divine connection to the grace of God that is upon the man of God:

He that receiveth a prophet in the name of a prophet shall receive a prophet's reward; and he that receiveth a righteous man in the name of a righteous man shall receive a righteous man's reward.

Matthew 10:41

There is a prophetic blessing that can only be provoked in this way. Your prosperity

173

is to comes through the prophets, but you must provoke it:

> *And they rose early in the morning, and went forth into the wilderness of Tekoa: and as they went forth, Jehoshaphat stood and said, Hear me, O Judah, and ye inhabitants of Jerusalem; Believe in the LORD your God, so shall ye be established; believe his prophets, so shall ye prosper.* 2 Chronicles 20:20

In Genesis 27:2-4, Isaac encouraged his firstborn to provoke God's blessing and assume the mantle of becoming a great nation. Esau despised it, but Jacob obeyed. Today, we have, not the nation of Abraham, but the nation of Israel (Jacob's new name).

The double portion of anointing did not come to Elisha merely because he was a Jew, but because he had faithfully served his master Elijah:

> *But Jehoshaphat said, Is there not here a prophet of the LORD, that we may*

enquire of the LORD by him? And one of the king of Israel's servants answered and said, Here is Elisha the son of Shaphat, which poured water on the hands of Elijah. 2 Kings 3:11

When what you have in your hand is not enough to do what you desire, put it in the hands of your prophet in faith, and in this way provoke your blessing.

The widow of Zarephath only had only a handful of flour and was preparing to die, but God sent the prophet her way, she gave to the prophet, and that ended her turmoil (see 1 Kings 17:10-16).

A Shunammite woman received a great miracle because of her giving heart to the prophet (see 2 Kings 4:8-17).

Paul wrote to the Philippian believers:

But I have all, and abound: I am full, having received of Epaphroditus the things which were sent from you, an odour of a sweet smell, a sacrifice accept-able, wellpleasing to God. But my God

shall supply all your need according to his riches in glory by Christ Jesus.
Philippians 4:18-19

Give To The Poor

The poor around you, most especially in the household of faith, present you with an opportunity to be blessed:

For ye have the poor always with you; but me ye have not always.
Matthew 26:11

Giving to the poor connects you to the King's treasury:

He that hath pity upon the poor lendeth unto the LORD; and that which he hath given will he pay him again.
Proverbs 19:17

If giving to the poor is lending to the Lord, He will surely pay you back:

Blessed is he that considereth the poor: the LORD will deliver him in time of trouble. The LORD will preserve him, and keep him alive; and he shall be blessed upon the earth: and thou wilt not deliver him unto the will of his enemies. Psalm 41:1-2

He that giveth unto the poor shall not lack: but he that hideth his eyes shall have many a curse. Proverbs 28:27

When Jesus walked the Earth, He showed compassion on the poor. When He said to Judas, the treasurer of His group of disciples, "What you are going to do do it quickly," the other disciples took it for granted that He was speaking of aiding the poor:

And after the sop Satan entered into him. Then said Jesus unto him, That thou doest, do quickly. Now no man at the table knew for what intent he spake this unto him. For some of them thought, because Judas had the bag,

177

> *that Jesus had said unto him, Buy those things that we have need of against the feast; or, that he should give something to the poor.* John 13:27-29

No kindness goes unnoticed in God's Kingdom.

3. **Provoke angelic intervention for wealth.** Never forget, when you have done the will of God, you will obtain the promise. The good news is that we have servants in the Kingdom that will establish God's mandate for us—if we care to use them:

> *Are they not all ministering spirits, sent forth to minister for them who shall be heirs of salvation?* Hebrews 1:14

> *Bless the LORD, ye his angels, that excel in strength, that do his commandments, hearkening unto the voice of his word.* Psalm 103:20

Angels are carriers of good news, and there is a good news on the way to you even now being brought by angels. I strongly believe that when Peter caught a fish with just enough money in its mouth to pay his and Jesus' taxes, it was the work of angels. Command them to go get your money. Your harvest is ripe, and they must bring it to you.

4. **Avoid unforgiveness and bitterness:** A defiled person cannot enjoy Kingdom wealth, meaning wealth with no pain attached to it.

> *Looking diligently lest any man fail of the grace of God; lest any root of bitterness springing up trouble you, and thereby many be defiled.* Hebrews 12:15

Jesus said, "Leave your offering at the altar and forgive your neighbor first":

> *Therefore if thou bring thy gift to the altar, and there rememberest that thy*

> *brother hath ought against thee; leave*
> *there thy gift before the altar, and go thy*
> *way; first be reconciled to thy brother,*
> *and then come and offer thy gift.*
>
> Matthew 5:23-24

5. **Receive grace now to apply the truth.** It is not the devil that is stopping you; it's you not listening to and/or obeying God's Spirit. Some have not yet realized that this is the key to unlimited blessings.

Why can you do all of this? Because you are now *In Charge!*

CHAPTER 4

LIVING PROOF

*For whatsoever is born of God overco-
meth the world: and this is the victory
that overcometh the world, even our
faith.*   1 John 5:4

Kingdom living is a life of victory and
not defeat. As children of the Kingdom, we
have the hosts of Heaven backing us in our
mandate on Earth, and that brings glory to
God through Christ Jesus.

Being able to overcome through Christ the
powers that be is the reason our victory in
life is unquestionable. Still, many have been
deceived. They take the tales of the enemy
for truth and relate with the world based on
human philosophies and discoveries. They

have forgotten that we have only discovered what already existed:

> *Don't let anyone capture you with empty philosophies and high-sounding nonsense that come from human thinking and from the spiritual powers of this world, rather than from Christ.* Colossians 2:8, NLT

You are not creating anything new, only discovering what has always been true. The Word tells us, *"Thanks be to God who gives us the victory through our Lord Jesus Christ"* (1 Corinthians 15:57, NKJV). We received our victory (conquest) as a gift from God through Christ. The victory is already there waiting for us; we just have to access it by faith.

If you don't have an understanding of the nature of the battle, how can you gain the victory? The Bible says that we are of God and the whole world lies in wickedness:

> *We know that we are of God, and the whole world lies under the sway of the wicked one.*   1 John 5:19, NKJV

Jesus said, *"In the world you will have tribulation"* (John 16:33, NKJV). However, as Psalm 110:1-3 reveals, we are destined to rule over our enemies:

> *The LORD said to my LORD,*
> *"Sit at My right hand,*
> *Till I make Your enemies Your footstool."*
> *The LORD shall send the rod of Your strength out of Zion.*
> *Rule in the midst of Your enemies!*
> *Your people shall be volunteers*
> *In the day of Your power;*
> *In the beauties of holiness, from the womb of the morning,*
> *You have the dew of Your youth.* (NKJV)

There are forces here on earth that want to limit our glory, but when we stand strong in Christ, they cannot succeed. In and through Christ Jesus, we are more than conquerors. The truth is that our victory is guaranteed because we are born of God. That is the final verdict. Getting the actualization of it comes through walking by faith.

The end times will reveal more of the evil acts of God's enemies. Therefore it is more important than ever that, as children of God, we take cover in the truth and know who we are, what we carry on the inside, and what our assignment on earth is:

> *Ye are of God, little children, and have overcome them: because greater is he that is in you, than he that is in the world.* 1 John 4:4

You and I have been fully armed against the wickedness of the world, but it is the discovery of this truth and our acting upon it that brings great manifestation. The cruelty of the enemy cannot "mess us up." Our covenant with God forbids it:

> *Have respect unto the covenant: for the dark places of the earth are full of the habitations of cruelty.* Psalm 74:20

This truth is not yet understood by many believers. They are constantly fighting the devil tooth and nail, and that is not the Gospel of Jesus Christ. If you are still fighting the devil, then Jesus did not finish His work. But He did finish it. Now all we have to fight is our own flesh and the fight of faith. If your faith is not in operation, then the devil takes over. Why? Because *"whatever is not from faith is sin"* (Romans 14:23, NKJV).

When God is not given His rightful place, the enemy takes over. Fight to know the truth, and your issues with Satan will be finished. Jesus Christ finished him:

Inasmuch then as the children have partaken of flesh and blood, He Himself likewise shared in the same, that through death He might destroy him who had the power of death, that is, the devil, and release those who through fear of death were all their lifetime subject to bondage. Hebrews 2:14-15, NKJV

Jesus said:

> *I saw Satan fall like lightning from heaven.* Luke 10:18, NKJV

And He never told us that Satan rose again. The enemy of your soul has been defeated, and it's time for you to walk in total victory in the name of Jesus Christ. Your joy, your peace, your health, and your destiny have all been paid for. Because Satan is now illegal, you have every right, by your legal standing in Christ, to cast him out in the name of Jesus Christ.

Before Jesus went to the cross, the enemy came to steal, kill, and destroy (see John 10:10), but through the cross, he lost that power over anyone who believes in the finished work of Christ. Now Satan can only take advantage of our ignorance. He uses wiles, fear, misinformation, and misinterpretation of the Scriptures to do his job. That is why Paul wrote to the Ephesian believers:

> *Put on the whole armour of God, that ye may be able to stand against the wiles of the devil.* Ephesians 6:11

And he wrote to the Corinthian church:

Lest Satan should get an advantage of us: for we are not ignorant of his devices.   2 Corinthians 2:11

According to the *Oxford Language Dictionary*, this word *wiles* means "devious or cunning stratagems employed in manipulating or persuading someone to do what one wants." The word *devices* refers to "mind games" and has to do with the way we think. If Satan can confuse your thinking, he can win a round or two.

THE IMPORTANCE OF FASTING AND PRAYER

One of the ways of overcoming the mind games of the enemy and retaining your victory is through fasting and prayer. This is one of the most powerful instruments for winning life's battles. Have you ever wondered why all the heroes of faith fasted and prayed? They were men and women of exploits, they got unusual results, and they ruled where others failed. We're talking about men and women like Moses, David, Daniel, Anna, Paul, Peter, and even our Lord Jesus Christ.

Why did these great heroes of the faith need to fast? Many want to have the same results they had, but they don't want to make the same sacrifices. As Jesus taught, there are results you cannot get on Earth without fasting and prayer:

> *If ye have faith as a grain of mustard seed, ye shall say unto this mountain, Remove hence to yonder place; and it shall remove; and nothing shall be impossible unto you. Howbeit this kind goeth not out but by prayer and fasting.*
> Matthew 17:20-21

We want the sun and moon to obey us, and we want to walk on water, but all these things are the results of sacrifice. Fasting and prayer subdue the flesh so that the spirit can take over.

Jesus said, *"When you fast"* (Matthew 6:16), not *if* you fast. Many believers are not seeing the maximum manifestation of their redemptive benefits because of their love for food.

The first Adam lost his position through food, and the last Adam got it back by neglect of food or fasting. Don't sell your birthright for food. Discipline yourself and get your spirit in tune with God:

> *Lest there be any fornicator, or profane person, as Esau, who for one morsel of meat sold his birthright.*
>
> Hebrews 12:16

You hear people saying, "Why should I fast? God is not wicked, and we are now under grace." Understand this truth: when you fast, you are not doing it for God. He doesn't need your fasting at all. You are the one who needs it.

Your flesh is accustomed to vanity and carnality, it wants its freedom, and it lives under the jurisdiction of the senses. The problem is that's where Satan dwells, and you can never defeat him on his own territory—never.

Fasting puts your flesh in check, so that you can connect with the Holy Spirit. If you are not fasting, you are not growing, you cannot manifest the power of God, and you cannot exercise your dominion. Just as we value prayer, we must also value fasting.

I strongly believe that when a situation is stubborn and seems to defy every other means, you need to do some fasting in order to connect with God's throne without any fleshy interference.

If your fasting is not intentional and focused, then it's not fasting; it's just dieting. Fasting is abstaining from food and pleasure for a purpose, and that purpose is to seek God. It's a sacrifice because you are putting God in the place of whatever you are accustomed to enjoying. This is an indication that He is all you need.

THE BENEFITS OF FASTING

1. **Access to the voice of the Lord:** You put a total end to frustration and defeat when

you hear the voice of the Lord concerning any matter.

> *The voice of the LORD is powerful; the voice of the LORD is full of majesty. The voice of the LORD breaketh the cedars; yea, the LORD breaketh the cedars of Lebanon.* Psalm 29:4-5

In Acts 13:2, the New Testament believers worshiped and fasted, and the voice of the Lord came to them with instructions for their destiny. It was the same in Old Testament times. Every time Israel was in jeopardy and some enemy was dominating them, they called for a fast and sought the face of God. The result was inevitable that God gave them a specific strategy, and when thy followed it, they won the battle. Now, it's your turn. This is your victory.

2. **Unusual favor:** Esther obtained favor instead of death through fasting and prayer (see Esther 4:16 and 5:2-3). When the early apostles needed to receive instructions

concerning their assignment, they fasted (see Acts 13:1-3).

3. **Develop intimacy with God and gain power for your destiny:** Jesus said it like this:

> *Can ye make the children of the bride-chamber fast, while the bridegroom is with them? But the days will come, when the bridegroom shall be taken away from them, and then shall they fast in those days.* Luke 5:34-35

With fasting and prayer, your spiritual capacity increases, your flesh diminishes, and you frustrate the devil. The devil wants to come in through your flesh, but when you silence the flesh through fasting, he is foiled.

If you fast and pray, God speaks to you and you receive guidance and direction. Stop feeding only the flesh, and start feeding your spirit. If you feel empty or lonely, your flesh is always controlling you, and the situation you are facing looks insurmountable, engage the instrument of prayer and fasting and you will be amazed by what God does.

Through fasting and prayer, Jesus prepared over a period of forty days for a ministry that lasted just three and a half years (see Luke 4:1-2 and 14). You, too, can *"return in the power of the Spirit"* after fasting.

4. **Receive revelation and divine understanding:** There is a thin line like a wall between the realm of the Spirit and the natural, and you can pull the flesh down through fasting and prayer to enter into that Spirit realm and receive revelation.

The Word of God is coded, so that the flesh cannot understand it (see 1 Corinthians 2:14). When you enter into the Spirit realm through fasting, your understanding is quickened (see Isaiah 58:6-9). No wonder Paul the apostle had such a great revelation that the world cannot stop admiring it. He fasted often (see 2 Corinthians 11:27).

Daniel requested time to fast and pray so that he could receive an answer from God (see Daniel 2:16-19).

Relying on God's Vengeance

We have enough tools in our hand to frustrate the enemy, as we are gaining speed and height in Jesus' name. Understand this: the comfort and glory of Zion comes by the vengeance of the Lord. This is God silencing all the enemies of the Church by divine judgement:

> *For it is the day of the LORD's vengeance, and the year of recompences for the controversy of Zion.*   Isaiah 34:8

This is when God changes our mourning into dancing, when *"the rod of the wicked"* is removed from *"the lot of the righteous"* by a divine hand (Psalm 125:3), when the terrible day of the Lord comes against the manifestation of every wickedness. It is not just the *vengeance* of the Lord; it also comes with *recompences*, meaning there will be rewards for any and all suffering on your part. You can experience this today in Jesus' name.

Never forget that the prophetic destiny of the Church is to be set above everything else:

> *And it shall come to pass in the last days, that the mountain of the LORD's house shall be established in the top of the mountains, and shall be exalted above the hills; and all nations shall flow unto it.* Isaiah 2:2

It is the vengeance of the Lord that will overcome everything that rises against the prophetic destiny of the Church. The days of sickness and oppression are over in the name of Jesus Christ.

Never forget: God is a jealous God, and He won't allow anyone to take His place in the life of His children. He said to Moses, *"Say unto Pharaoh, Israel is my son"* (Exodus 4:22). You, too, are a son [or daughter] of God:

> *But as many as received him, to them gave he power to become the sons of God, even to them that believe on his name.* John 1:12

Whatever has been holding you in captivity, whatever has been delaying your joy must go, for God is not the author of it. These are of the enemy, but God's vengeance is released upon them now in the name of Jesus Christ:

> *If I whet my glittering sword, and mine hand take hold on judgment; I will render vengeance to mine enemies, and will reward them that hate me.*
>
> Deuteronomy 32:41

> *For we know him that hath said, Vengeance belongeth unto me, I will recompense, saith the Lord. And again, The Lord shall judge his people.*
>
> Hebrews 10:30

There are destinies that will never be fulfilled and dreams that will never manifest until God shows up.

Lucifer put himself forward as being equal to God and attempted to replace God:

How art thou fallen from heaven, O Lucifer, son of the morning! how art thou cut down to the ground, which didst weaken the nations! For thou hast said in thine heart, I will ascend into heaven, I will exalt my throne above the stars of God: I will sit also upon the mount of the congregation, in the sides of the north: I will ascend above the heights of the clouds; I will be like the most High. Yet thou shalt be brought down to hell, to the sides of the pit.

Isaiah 14:12-15

What did God say to all of this: *"Instead, you will be brought down to the place of the dead, down to its lowest depths." "You have been thrown down to the earth, you who destroyed the nations of the world"* (NLT). That was Satan's end.

The psalmist declared:

Let God arise, let his enemies be scattered: let them also that hate him flee before him.   Psalm 68:1

God Himself has declared that He will be the enemy of our enemies and the adversary of our adversaries (see Exodus 23:220). He has also said:

> *Say to them that are of a fearful heart, Be strong, fear not: behold, your God will come with vengeance, even God with a recompence; he will come and save you.*
> Isaiah 35:4

This is not preached nearly enough, and that's why we don't all know it. Jesus asked the question:

> *When the Son of man cometh, shall he find faith on the earth?*   Luke 18:8

We might add, Shall He find faith in His vengeance? Far too many of us only know Him as the God of love; we don't know Him as the God of vengeance. Those who connived to put Daniel in the den of lions did not themselves escape. Instead, they were thrown to the lions and were then eaten. In the same way, every unjust treatment you have suffered will be avenged by a divine visitation. God has said:

> *Vengeance is mine; I will repay, saith the Lord.* Romans 12:19

Yes, we are to forgive those who have wronged us. Yes, we are to love our enemies, and we are to pray for those who despitefully use us. But that does not negate God's vengeance. He will have vengeance upon our enemies.

God's vengeance has nothing to do with hatred, retaliation, or resentment. It is a part of His love for justice. It is setting things straight. It is fulfilling a divine agenda. It is God going ahead of His people to fight their cause because the system of this world is against them.

When any man or any thing stands in the way of God's purpose, His vengeance is triggered. He said:

> *Fury is not in me: who would set the briers and thorns against me in battle?*

> *I would go through them, I would burn them together.*　　　Isaiah 27:4

The laws and systems of this world were set in place to hinder our Kingdom assignment, but God is revealing Himself today in vengeance.

The mandate of the covenant we have with God is this:

> *I will bless them that bless thee, and curse him that curseth thee: and in thee shall all families of the earth be blessed.*
> Genesis 12:3

Anyone who sets himself as an enemy of that covenant will be dealt with by God Himself. Abimelech, the king of the Philistines, crossed the line, and God struck him with swift vengeance (see Genesis 20:3, 7, and 17-18). We, as heirs of Abraham, are now the inheritors of the covenant:

> *And if ye be Christ's, then are ye Abraham's seed, and heirs according to the promise.*　　　Galatians 3:29

Therefore, God is striking today on our behalf, for we are under the same covenant. Get ready for compensation. Without God's vengeance, the manifestation of His glory will not be realized.

The purpose of the vengeance of God is to promote, protect, and advance you as you pursue your God-given assignment in the Kingdom. Jesus said:

> *For these be the days of vengeance, that all things which are written may be fulfilled.* Luke 21:22

All that has been written about you and me must now be fulfilled. As Isaiah foretold:

> *The Spirit of the LORD God is upon me; because the LORD hath anointed me to preach good tidings unto the meek; he hath sent me to bind up the brokenhearted, to proclaim liberty to the captives, and the opening of the prison to them that are bound; to proclaim the acceptable year*

> *of the LORD, and the day of vengeance of our God; to comfort all that mourn; to appoint unto them that mourn in Zion, to give unto them beauty for ashes, the oil of joy for mourning, the garment of praise for the spirit of heaviness; that they might be called trees of righteousness, the planting of the LORD, that he might be glorified.* Isaiah 61:1-3

Jesus fulfilled these words, and we can too:

> *The Spirit of the Lord is upon me, because he hath anointed me to preach the gospel to the poor; he hath sent me to heal the brokenhearted, to preach deliverance to the captives, and recovering of sight to the blind, to set at liberty them that are bruised, to preach the acceptable year of the Lord.* Luke 4:18-19

After Herod killed all the children from two years and under, the judgement of God came upon him (see Matthew 2:19-20).

When Jesus was grown and walked the Earth as a man, He did not take vengeance into His own hands. He allowed the Holy Spirit, the Messenger of the covenant, to take care of it on His behalf.

When Ananias and Sapphira conspired to lie to the early apostles, those apostles didn't have to take action themselves. The Spirit immediately struck Ananias and Sapphira dead (see Acts 5).

PROVOKING GODS VENGEANCE

The law of the Spirit (see Romans 8:1-2) can be provoked by engaging it by faith. How do we do this? Here are some guidelines:

1. **Service:** When you serve God, your enemy is in trouble, and you frustrate his plans (see, for example, Numbers 10:7-12 and Isaiah 41:9-12).

2. **Sacrifice:** A sacrificial offering can bring the vengeance of God upon your adversaries and discomfit them (see 1 Samuel 7:8-11).

3. **Prayer:** Enough is enough! When you cry out, God shows up (see Acts 13:9-12 and Psalm 94:1-5).

4. **Praise:** When you choose to worship God in the face of any enemy attack, a recompense follows (see 2 Chronicles 20:22-25).

THE BENEFITS OF GOD'S VENGEANCE

1. **It brings supernatural breakthroughs:** (see, for example, Exodus 11:1, and Esther before Modecai, Esther 7:9-10 and 8:2).

2. **It strengthens our confidence:** God can't stand the oppression of His children (see, for example, Luke 18:7-8 and Genesis 12:3).

3. **It comes with a guarantee that your dream will come to pass:** (see, for example, Jeremiah 30:19 and Isaiah 45:2-3)

To activate God's vengeance on your behalf, pray prayers like these:

- O God of vengeance, show Yourself now on my behalf today. Enough is enough! You are all I have. Jesus, help me now with my health, finances, marriage, children, etc.

- Father, in the name of Jesus Christ, whatever is impeding the release of my portion, be removed now, in the name of Jesus.

- Father, in the name of Jesus Christ, for everything I have lost, let there be a recompense today. Before this day is over, I will recover all.

You cannot operate in the ways of God and not create waves here on Earth. You cannot operate in the ways of God and not become the envy of your world.

UNDERSTANDING THE WAYS OF GOD

God said very clearly through Isaiah:

> *For my thoughts are not your thoughts,*
> *neither are your ways my ways, saith*
> *the LORD. For as the heavens are higher*
> *than the earth, so are my ways higher*
> *than your ways, and my thoughts than*
> *your thoughts.*   Isaiah 55:8-9

Your level of results changes when you begin to operate in God's ways, not your own opinion. Your opinion may be good, but it is certainly too low to produce an enviable destiny. God, on the other hand, set the whole universe in place, so He knows what works and what produces outstanding results.

Marching around the city of Jericho for seven days did not make much sense to humans. It was like announcing, "We're here; come and kill us." But that was God's way, and when the Israelites obeyed, the walls came down, and they won the battle. God's Word changes you because it represents His way of doing things.

You need no longer be part of struggling majority. Why? Because the Owner of the

Universe has placed you at the center of His plan, and with Him all things are possible. We have been translated into a Kingdom where victory is our identity, and failure is impossible ... unless you make that your choice. Because we are born of God, we overcome the world:

> *For whatsoever is born of God overcometh the world: and this is the victory that overcometh the world, even our faith.* 1 John 5:4

We are called to sit with Jesus in heavenly places, and that is a sovereign rule, the peak of authority and dominion. That is the place of victory, the throne room, where decisions concerning the Universe are made. On that seat, we laugh at the enemy. We don't cry. The psalmist declared:

> *Why do the heathen rage, and the people imagine a vain thing? The kings of the earth set themselves, and the rulers take counsel together, against the LORD, and*

> *against his anointed, saying, Let us break*
> *their bands asunder, and cast away their*
> *cords from us. He that sitteth in the heav-*
> *ens shall laugh: the LORD shall have them*
> *in derision.* Psalm 2:1-4

You can't afford to keep looking down, when everyone and everything including the devil is looking up to you:

> *Behold, what manner of love the Father*
> *hath bestowed upon us, that we should*
> *be called the sons of God: therefore the*
> *world knoweth us not, because it knew*
> *him not.* 1 John 3:1

Sons of God ... that is the highest level of elevation. It is not because of our own ability but because of His love. That makes us superior to everyone in the flesh:

> *Which were born, not of blood, nor of the*
> *will of the flesh, nor of the will of man,*
> *but of God.* John 1:13

We put our minds on our body far too much, and the result is that our bodies get weaker because of the burden of our work. We need to keep our mind on Jesus, and He will keep us *"in perfect peace"*:

> *Thou wilt keep him in perfect peace, whose mind is stayed on thee: because he trusteth in thee.*   Isaiah 26:3

When your mind is at peace, your body will follow. The reason people are tired and sick is because their mind is on their body. When the mind is completely placed on God, He takes over.

Understand that there is nothing inferior or weak about the Body of Christ. We have overcome the flesh, sin, sickness, disease, and Satan. We have been transformed and translated into the glorious image of Christ on Earth. The power of His righteousness and the presence of the Holy Spirit have so filled our bodies that those bodies have no place to feel weak or sick ... unless we are listening to the deception of the enemy:

> *And the work of righteousness shall be peace; and the effect of righteousness quietness and assurance for ever. And my people shall dwell in a peaceable habitation, and in sure dwellings, and in quiet resting places.* Isaiah 32:17-18

The sons of God are holy and temperate, and they excel in all things. They must be heard, for they are filled with wisdom.

Even sin has been destroyed in the flesh, so that it cannot lord over you any more. If God condemned sin in the flesh, then sickness and diseases that dwell in the flesh must also go:

> *Likewise reckon ye also yourselves to be dead indeed unto sin, but alive unto God through Jesus Christ our Lord.*
> *For sin shall not have dominion over you: for ye are not under the law, but under grace.* Romans 6:11 and 14

> *Whosoever abideth in him sinneth not: whosoever sinneth hath not seen him,*

neither known him. Little children, let no man deceive you: he that doeth righteousness is righteous, even as he is righteous. He that committeth sin is of the devil; for the devil sinneth from the beginning. For this purpose the Son of God was manifested, that he might destroy the works of the devil.

1 John 3:6-8

REJECT FEAR

The enemy of your victory is fear. Fear is repetitive and intensive. It is a negative emotion that must not be allowed. When fear takes over, victory is lost. Why? Because fear has torment:

There is no fear in love; but perfect love casteth out fear: because fear hath torment. He that feareth is not made perfect in love. 1 John 4:18

All fear is based on what God has not said. It has been whispered to us by the devil. The

211

purpose of fear is to remove your confidence and make you vulnerable and miserable. Fear puts you at the center of everything and shows you how weak you are to handle it. You will never find anyone who depends on himself or herself who does not fall victim to fear. God knew that would happen, and that is why He has assured you:

I will never leave thee, nor forsake thee.
Hebrews 13:5

God has consistently said to His children, "Fear not. Do not be dismayed. I am with you" (see, for instance, Joshua 10:25). Keep the door to fear closed by hearing and obeying His commands. You can do all things through Christ, the Hope of Glory, who is in you. You are not alone, so why should you fight alone? You carry all the features of God in you:

But as many as received Him, to them
He gave the right to become children of
God, to those who believe in His name:

who were born, not of blood, nor of the
will of the flesh, nor of the will of man,
but of God.   John 1:12-13

When worry, stress, procrastination, or lack of confidence in your potential comes, it is an indication that you are under the influence of fear. Fear says, "You don't deserve this," "You'll get hurt," "What if it never happens?" "You are not good enough!" This is what it's like to be caught in the web of fear. Change that attitude, and begin to walk in faith, and those voices will be stilled.

You can never defeat fear with fear. You must confront your fear with the Word of God and get rid of it.

Recognizing your fear is not a sign of defeat; it is a recognition of what you are facing. If you fail to face your inner fears, you cannot overcome what hinders you.

In the time of Gideon, God said to him, "Whoever is fearful and afraid should go back." Out of 32,000 soldiers, 22,000 turned around and went home that day. Wow!

> *Now therefore go to, proclaim in the*
> *ears of the people, saying, Whosoever*
> *is fearful and afraid, let him return and*
> *depart early from mount Gilead. And*
> *there returned of the people twenty and*
> *two thousand; and there remained ten*
> *thousand.* Judges 7:3

You can overcome fear and defeat when you have an image of victory on the inside. We are where we are because God makes it happen for His glory and our good, and there is greatness on the inside of you, but fear can kill that greatness:

> *For whatsoever is born of God overco-*
> *meth the world: and this is the victory*
> *that overcometh the world, even our*
> *faith.* 1 John 5:4

Fear will sap your strength and energy and leave you with weakness. If you cannot overcome your fear, you cannot stop your opposition. If you stop pushing with faith, you allow fear to take over. If you are in a class with the gods, why should you lose in the realm of the natural?

I have said, Ye are gods; and all of you are children of the most High.

Psalm 82:6

Never forget that whatever you face in life wants to and will intimidate you ... if you allow it:

The fear of man bringeth a snare: but whoso putteth his trust in the Lord *shall be safe.* Proverbs 29:25

For ye have not received the spirit of bondage again to fear; but ye have received the Spirit of adoption, whereby we cry, Abba, Father. Romans 8:15

Now when they saw the boldness of Peter and John, and perceived that they were unlearned and ignorant men, they marvelled; and they took knowledge of them, that they had been with Jesus. Acts 4:13

Do you remember Goliath? He had an entire army trembling before him ... that is until David stepped up. You, too, are in the world to win, so what are you afraid of? Whatever confronts you, the Greater One inside you is never tired. So, why should you be?

To be fearless and to be arrogant are two completely different things. Don't be arrogant and think you are fearless. To be arrogant is not to prepare and think you are in charge. Action and preparation will stop fear any day. God has not given us the spirit of fear. Rise up against fear, for you are wired for victory.

Sickness, disease, poverty, and failure cannot overcome you. You have been ordained by God to overcome them all. Rise up now, for it's time for victory. You are living proof. Hallelujah! Boldly declare:

1. Father, thank You for divine placement in Your plan and purpose in the name of Jesus Christ. I have victory over you, Satan, according to the Word of God. I have victory

over sin, sickness and disease, poverty, and oppression, so I bind you now and declare, "Get out of my life and come back no more in Jesus Christ's name."

2. Father, in the name of Jesus Christ, I come against the spirit of fear. You will not have dominion over me. God has given me the spirit of love, power, and a sound mind, and that's what I have now in Jesus' name.

3. Father, in the name of Jesus Christ, let Your Word be real to me. Fill me with Your Spirit and a passion for the lost. Change my story today in Jesus' name.

The Church is the beauty of Creation. She is the wonder of the Earth:

> *Beautiful for situation, the joy of the whole earth, is mount Zion, on the sides of the north, the city of the great King.*
> Psalm 48:2

THE CHURCH, THE INSTRUMENT OF RULERSHIP

Everything God put under Christ is for the benefit of the Church:

> *God has put all things under the author-*
> *ity of Christ and has made him head over*
> *all things for the benefit of the church.*
> Ephesians 1:22, NLT

It takes understanding to see this. Cancer is under Christ, so it's under you, along with diabetes, high blood pressure, and corona-virus. You must not forget what Jesus said:

> *And Jesus came and spake unto them,*
> *saying, All power is given unto me in*
> *heaven and in earth. Go ye therefore,*
> *and teach all nations, baptizing them in*
> *the name of the Father, and of the Son,*
> *and of the Holy Ghost: teaching them*
> *to observe all things whatsoever I have*
> *commanded you: and, lo, I am with you*

always, even unto the end of the world.
Amen. Matthew 28:18-20

Since all power has been given unto you, you are in charge. Take dominion just as the sun takes dominion over the day, and the moon takes dominion over the night. Nothing can torment you or stop you.

When the enemy sows his seeds of fear, the moment you hear it, see it, and feel it, it takes you out of the Spirit realm and brings you to a mental realm where you meditate on how bad things are. All the attention of the heavens are upon you, and you can never be a victim ... if you take responsibility:

> *All praise to God, the Father of our Lord Jesus Christ, who has blessed us with every spiritual blessing in the heavenly realms because we are united with Christ. Even before he made the world, God loved us and chose us in Christ to be holy and without fault in his eyes.*
>
> Ephesians 1:3-4, NLT

There is enough provision for every single one of us. It inexhaustible, and it is ours because the coming of Jesus Christ gave us access. Everything we missed in the garden has been restored back to us:

> *I also pray that you will understand the incredible greatness of God's power for us who believe him. This is the same mighty power that raised Christ from the dead and seated him in the place of honor at God's right hand in the heavenly realms.* Ephesians 1:19-20, NLT

There is a need for expectation, confidence, and a determination to take what is already there waiting for collection by faith. The blood already gave us the access to everything. We therefore have boldness:

> *Let us therefore come boldly unto the throne of grace, that we may obtain mercy, and find grace to help in time of need.* Hebrews 4:16

Never forget: we are called to be filled with all the fullness of God:

> *And to know the love of Christ, which pass-eth knowledge, that ye might be filled with all the fulness of God.* Ephesians 3:19

Wow! That's too much. It gives you the divine capacity to walk in a new anointing and experience miracles every day. Please determine to serve God with all your strength, for you have nothing to lose. It will all be gain for you. The Bible says *"no good thing will he withhold from them that walk uprightly"*:

> *For the LORD God is a sun and shield: the LORD will give grace and glory: no good thing will he withhold from them that walk uprightly.* Psalm 84:11

If we unleash the Greater One inside of us, the lesser and smaller ones on earth will be swallowed up. There are heights in God's plan for you that God knows you can't ever get to by your own strength and ability. His extravagant grace is given to you to achieve far beyond your expectations through faith in the incorruptible Word of God.

The Law of the Spirit of life in Christ Jesus, has brought you and me into total victory, no matter what Hell does. Satan does not have dominion over you. You are not under that government. There has been a complete change of government, and you are now under a new law. You cannot remain a victim when the power of the world to come resides in you now:

> *For it is impossible for those who were once enlightened, and have tasted of the heavenly gift, and were made partakers of the Holy Ghost, and have tasted the good word of God, and the powers of the world to come, if they shall fall away, to renew them again unto repentance; seeing they crucify to themselves the Son of God afresh, and put him to an open shame.* Hebrews 6:4-6

We are not waiting to get to heaven to be empowered and rule. Our reign starts right here and right now. I want you to come to the place that you know you cannot be moved. You are unshakable. The righteous shall never be moved:

> *Cast thy burden upon the* Lord, *and he shall sustain thee: he shall never suffer the righteous to be moved.*
>
> Psalm 55:22

Those of us who are in Christ are unshakable. We may experience natural things on a daily basis, but we belong to a realm that rules the natural by the power of the Spirit through the Word of the living God.

Romans 8:9 declares of believers:

> *But ye are not in the flesh, but in the Spirit, if so be that the Spirit of God dwell in you.*

You cannot lose. You cannot be "messed up." You are one with Christ, and His Spirit dwells in you.

Understand this: whatever brings failure, sickness, and diseases is of the devil, and the devil has been defeated for your sake. You have abundant life to reign over him forever. If you see the devil, don't be afraid. Know that he has been defeated, and it's your turn to take over. You are *In Charge!*

The psalmist sang:

> *Who satisfies your mouth with good things...* Psalm 103:5

Our victory and the wonders God performs in our daily life is to prove what He can do for and with mortal man, what His grace is capable of doing with any man or woman who will unite with Christ Jesus. We are fully in charge of running this planet, and that is called grace:

> *For he raised us from the dead along with Christ and seated us with him in the heavenly realms because we are united with Christ Jesus. So God can*

point to us in all future ages as examples
of the incredible wealth of his grace and
kindness toward us, as shown in all he
has done for us who are united with
Christ Jesus.   Ephesians 2:6-7, NLT

God can point to us and say, "This is what My grace produces." Oh, hallelujah! Your miracle is established through the following principles:

1. **Believe in the love of God**: Many have believed in God, but relatively few have believed in His love. Without faith in His love, you will lose your confidence when you are tried. God is powerful, but that is not His name. His name is Love (see 1 John 4:8, and 16-17).

With faith in God's love, boldness comes to you, and you know you will never be left alone. God will and must show up for you because He loves you. You, however, must believe in His love.

The story of the prodigal son shows that the father will bless you and rescue you irrespective of your situation ... if and when you come back home. David said, *"Though I walk through the valley of the shadow of death, I will fear no evil: for thou art with me"* (Psalm 23:4). Hallelujah! Miracles must come to you because Daddy loves you. See His love for you in Psalm 103:8-14. Fear Him, and you are showing your love for Him. How do you know you love Him?

You Love His Word

(See Psalm 119:11, 162, and Job 23:12)

You Love His House

(See Psalm 122:1, 69:9, and 119:165)

David said, *"I had rather be a doorkeeper in the house of my God, than to dwell in the tents of wickedness"* (Psalm 84:10.

You Love His People

(See Hebrews 10:25, Psalm 133:1-2, and Galatians 6:10)

You Love Souls

This is what cost God His only Son. God loves souls because He loves Himself (see John 3:16), and when you are of God, you will also love souls. God will pay anything to get Himself back. When you allow people to go to Hell, you have cut a part of God off and given it to Satan for destruction. Go and rescue them. No wonder Jesus said, "I will go with you." Be committed to winning souls.

2. **Believe in the Word of God:** The truth that we must realize is that God's Word and God's personality cannot be separated. Wherever you see God, you see His Word. God's Word is a person; it's not letters on a page (see John 1:1-3). Convince yourself that the Word of God is the final say over your life, irrespective of how you feel. Then, whatever He asks you to do, do it (see John 2:5 and Psalm 138:2).

God has magnified His Word above His name. Therefore, we must also put His

Word first. The prophet said to the leper, "Go to the Jordan and wash." It was not medicine. It was the Word that cleansed him of leprosy. Don't use your situation to explain God's Word; use the Word to explain your situation (see Matthew 24:35).

3. **Act on the spoken Word:** You cannot believe the Word and not act on it. The reason you argue and get frustrated is because you don't believe. The woman with the issue of blood said in her heart, *"If I may but touch his garment, I shall be whole"* (Matthew 9:21). However, she didn't just think it; she acted on it and was made whole. Her faith was sparked by hearing about Jesus. (See Mark 5:27-29 and Mark 16:17-18.

Start rejoicing, and act on your faith. Bring all the tithes to the storehouse. Then, when you have brought them, give God thanks and be expectant, for the promised blessing is on its way.

4. **Believe the prophet God sent to you:** Prophets are divine agents of God

in human form. They are a gift from God to you. They unravel the secrets of God to take you to your destiny. However, their ministry is useless if you won't believe them. (See Hosea 12:13, 2 Chronicles 20:20b and Ephesians 4:11-14).

You will know prophets by their fruit. Stick with them and obey the instructions they bring, and you will find that God is committed to honoring the Word they speak (see Isaiah 44:26).

5. **Declare the spoken word:** (See Numbers 14:28)

> *We having the same spirit of faith, according as it is written, I believed, and therefore have I spoken; we also believe, and therefore speak.*
>
> 2 Corinthians 4:13

Your declaration releases God's power for performance.

6. **Thank God for the miracle in anticipation of it:** (See Philippians 4:6 and Romans 4:20).

Father in the name of Jesus Christ, I believe Your Word. I receive my miracle now. I take my healing and my deliverance in the name of Jesus Christ. Jesus Christ, touch me now. Father, I receive Your wisdom in the name of Jesus Christ.

Why can you do all of this? Because you are now *In Charge!*

CHAPTER 5

LIVING IN A WORLD OF WONDERS

He sent a man before them, even Joseph, who was sold for a servant: whose feet they hurt with fetters: he was laid in iron: until the time that his word came: the word of the LORD tried him.

The king sent and loosed him; even the ruler of the people, and let him go free. He made him lord of his house, and ruler of all his substance: to bind his princes at his pleasure; and teach his senators wisdom. Psalm 105:17-22

There is nothing that distinguishes destiny like the revelation of the Word of God. You can't walk in revelation and not live in admiration. A dream was revealed to Daniel in a night vision, and he became the governor of Babylon (see Daniel 2:19). It is the revealed Word that changes your status, not your own efforts. Joseph was in chains until the word came to him. Then the chains were broken, and elevation came. Let the eyes of your understanding be opened to these truths even now in Jesus' name.

> *Enter with the password: "Thank you!"*
> *Make yourselves at home, talking praise.*
> *Thank him. Worship him.*
>
> Psalm 100:4, MSG

The key to the presence of God is praise and thanksgiving. If you don't see that, your struggle will continue. This has nothing to do with your opinion and views; it is a Kingdom mystery. The man who killed Goliath and became king moved up from a shepherd status. He won all his battles because he had learned to praise God. He even said that death could not hold him bound because of God's presence (see Psalm 23:4). He obtained all through praise and thanksgiving. It is when you obey the command that you become a commander.

Why do we praise God? Because He is worthy of our praise. Through His mercy our sins were completely blotted out, as if we had never committed them in the first place:

> *Come now, and let us reason together, saith the LORD: though your sins be as scarlet, they shall be as white as snow; though they be red like crimson, they shall be as wool.* Isaiah 1:18

What makes man a slave in the hands of the devil is sin. Jesus could not be enslaved because there was no sin in Him. He said the prince of this world had come to Him and found nothing:

> *Hereafter I will not talk much with you: for the prince of this world cometh, and hath nothing in me.* John 14:30

Because of this, Jesus ruled the Universe as the holy and righteous One of God. Knowing that you and I could not produce what was required to make us a saint and righteous before God, He took our sin away on His own account. He paid the price for us, and you are now free before God. You are master over Satan, bearing no guilt whatsoever:

> *Yet now he has reconciled you to himself through the death of Christ in his physical body. As a result, he has brought you into his own presence, and you are holy and blameless as you stand before him without a single fault.*
>
> Colossians 1:22, NLT

When a photographer takes your photograph, he then takes it to his studio and edits it. He removes spots and blemishes, inserts a more appealing background, and his touch of excellence is so great that you might not even recognize yourself.

That is exactly what God does for us through the blood of Jesus Christ. He removes every blemish and gives us a face-lift. Satan himself cannot believe it's you. There is no fault, no blemish at all. That's why we give God praise. He alone is worthy.

Colossians 2:10 tells us that we are complete in Him now. That should give you the boldness needed to approach God's presence. If you acknowledge that fact, you will praise Him forever.

I am not in bondage to anything. Why? Because Jesus stands in God's presence for me as my Advocate, my Attorney. With Him, I cannot lose a case. I give Him thanks, and that brings me to His presence.

He inhabits the praises of His people:

> *Still, You are holy; You make Your home on the praises of Israel.*
> Psalm 22:3, The Voice

God's presence changes things:

1. **In God's presence things blossom:** Nothing is permitted to dry up or die in God's presence. Remember the rod of Aaron

(see Numbers 17:7-8). God's presence makes all the difference. It is His presence that makes a common believer a conqueror.

Things tremble when God shows up. As you learn to praise God, you will blossom and bear fruit. Praise God on purpose instead of complaining. If things are not yet working for you, know that God has a plan for you, and He is working in the background. Whatever you do, don't stop praising Him.

2. **In God's presence, there is victory:** The presence of God was tied to the Ark of the Covenant in old testament days. When Israel took the Ark into battle, victory was certain:

> *And when the ark of the covenant of the LORD came into the camp, all Israel shouted with a great shout, so that the earth rang again. And when the Philistines heard the noise of the shout, they said, What meaneth the noise of this great shout in the camp of the*

Hebrews? And they understood that the ark of the LORD was come into the camp. And the Philistines were afraid, for they said, God is come into the camp. And they said, Woe unto us! for there hath not been such a thing heretofore. Woe unto us! who shall deliver us out of the hand of these mighty Gods? these are the Gods that smote the Egyptians with all the plagues in the wilderness.

1 Samuel 4:5-8

God used that Ark to humiliate His enemies. One day the Philistines captured the Ark and took it into the house of their god, Dagon. Amazingly, what they intended as a humiliation to Israel and her God turned into a total humiliation for them and their god (see 1 Samuel 5:1-5). When you continue in praise, no enemy will ever be able to overcome you.

Why do we enter God's presence with praise? This is the same presence that parted the waters of the Red Sea. *"The sea saw it and fled"*:

> *When Israel went out of Egypt, the house of Jacob from a people of strange language; Judah was his sanctuary, and Israel his dominion. The sea saw it, and fled: Jordan was driven back.*
>
> Psalm 114:1-3

3. **In God's presence, there is no shame or reproach:** When you live in the presence of God, there is a total end to shame and error. Israel erred. They took the Ark of the Covenant and put it on a cart to transport it. As they went, the cart shook, and the Ark was about to fall. A man named Uzzah reached out to rescue it. Touching that sacred piece of Tabernacle furniture, however was forbidden and God smote him:

> *And they set the ark of God upon a new cart, and brought it out of the house of Abinadab that was in Gibeah: and Uzzah and Ahio, the sons of Abinadab, drave the new cart.*
> *And when they came to Nachon's threshingfloor, Uzzah put forth his hand*

to the ark of God, and took hold of it; for the oxen shook it. And the anger of the LORD was kindled against Uzzah; and God smote him there for his error; and there he died by the ark of God.

1 Samuel 6:4-7

In the midst of praise, God judges error, and no shame is allowed. Every error against your destiny is judged this day.

4. **In God's presence, there is fullness of joy**: God's presence provokes joy, which is a necessary ingredient for victory:

Thou wilt shew me the path of life: in thy presence is fulness of joy; at thy right hand there are pleasures for evermore.

Psalm 16:11

You need joy to draw water from the wells of salvation:

Therefore with joy shall ye draw water out of the wells of salvation. Isaiah 12:3

God is up to the task, and whatever comes, in does not matter. He will not mismanage my life. Whatever happens, I am winning. This causes joy to spring up in our hearts and inspires even more praise.

Father God sees me the way He sees Jesus. I am not a failure. Victory is mine. Hallelujah!

5. **In God's presence, you will never stink or become obsolete, never:** When God gave His children manna in the wilderness, it was like bread raining down from Heaven. He told Moses to take some of it for a memorial and place it in the Ark of the Covenant. That manna remained there for the next forty years (see Hebrews 9:4). Still, after all that time, it was not rancid or stale, and it had no odor. Why? Because it was in the preserving presence of God. You must be conscious of this need for God's presence today, for your time of refreshing has come:

Repent ye therefore, and be converted, that your sins may be blotted out, when

*the times of refreshing shall come from
the presence of the Lord.*   Acts 3:19

Step into the wonders of praise, and
change your story today in Jesus' name.

Life is bumpy and frustrating without the
supernatural. You and I are called into the
supernatural because we are actually repre-
senting the supernatural world here in the
natural world. Jesus said:

*The wind bloweth where it listeth, and
thou hearest the sound thereof, but canst
not tell whence it cometh, and whither
it goeth: so is every one that is born of
the Spirit.*   John 3:8

This is the realm you are called to live
in. The world will pay attention to us
only when they see something unusual.
Something about David brought him to the
attention of King Saul:

*And the king said, Enquire thou whose
son the stripling is.*   1 Samuel 17:56

What was it that so impressed the king? It was the death of the giant Goliath. This is the season of announcement for you. The world will be looking for you to excel by the hand of the Lord. You can no longer be ignored.

The supernatural is provoked and engaged through praise, for praise brings God into play. Of course, your praise must be genuine. When you praise without understanding, it is mere entertainment:

> *For God is the King of all the earth: sing ye praises with understanding.* Psalm 47:7

When people sing and dance before God in worship with understanding, that takes their case out of their own hands and puts it squarely in the hands of God. Why praise? It is His prescription. When you praise Him, you stir Him up, for praise glorifies God:

> *Whoso offereth praise glorifieth me: and to him that ordereth his conversation aright will I shew the salvation of God.*
> Psalm 50:23

When we praise God for who He is and what He has done, we provoke His intervention to do new things today and tomorrow:

> *Let the people praise thee, O God; let all the people praise thee.* Psalm 67:5

You cannot praise God and not experience an elevation. This is an unfailing principle of the Kingdom. When faith is released into the truth, freedom is always the result.

What comes to you when you praise God heartily?

1. **Access to the voice of the Lord:** The most powerful tool in the world of wonders is the voice of the Lord. His voice brings total victory and deliverance to His people. The Israelites were frustrated and in jeopardy. The Egyptians were behind them, and the Red Sea was before them. It looked like a dead-end. Then came the voice of the Lord, telling them to go forward. And what happened when they obeyed? The sea parted, and a pathway was made for them through the sea.

In Charge

> *Let us go up against Judah, and vex it,*
> *and let us make a breach therein for us,*
> *and set a king in the midst of it, even the*
> *son of Tabeal: thus saith the Lord God,*
> *It shall not stand, neither shall it come*
> *to pass.* Isaiah 7:6-7

The voice of the Lord will silence the voice of man and the counsel of the wicked, and your access to the voice of the Lord is through praise:

> *Ye shall have a song, as in the night*
> *when a holy solemnity is kept; and glad-*
> *ness of heart, as when one goeth with a*
> *pipe to come into the mountain of the*
> *Lord, to the mighty One of Israel. And*
> *the Lord shall cause his glorious voice*
> *to be heard, and shall shew the lighting*
> *down of his arm, with the indignation*
> *of his anger, and with the flame of a*
> *devouring fire, with scattering, and*
> *tempest, and hailstones. For through the*
> *voice of the Lord shall the Assyrian be*
> *beaten down, which smote with a rod.*
> Isaiah 30:29-31

Yes, this is where our victory is established:

The voice of the LORD is powerful; the voice of the LORD is full of majesty. The voice of the LORD breaketh the cedars; yea, the LORD breaketh the cedars of Lebanon. He maketh them also to skip like a calf; Lebanon and Sirion like a young unicorn. The voice of the LORD divideth the flames of fire. The voice of the LORD shaketh the wilderness; the LORD shaketh the wilderness of Kadesh. The voice of the LORD maketh the hinds to calve, and discovereth the forests: and in his temple doth every one speak of his glory.

Psalm 29:4-9

Just one word from the Lord can settle you forever.

At one point, there was famine everywhere. Things were all out of sorts. Then the voice of the Lord came:

Then Elisha said, Hear ye the word of the LORD; Thus saith the LORD, To

> *morrow about this time shall a measure*
> *of fine flour be sold for a shekel, and two*
> *measures of barley for a shekel, in the*
> *gate of Samaria.*   2 Kings 7:1

It happened because the voice of the Lord is creative and productive. It does not matter how difficult the situation, praise God unconditionally. Then expect to hear the voice of the Lord for direction.

2. **The power to do wonders:** When Christianity is stripped of wonders, it has been reduced to the status of any ordinary religion. God instituted a mystery that makes you a wonder to your world. You manifest and see wonders in and through praise.

> *Who is like unto thee, O Lord, among*
> *the gods? who is like thee, glorious in*
> *holiness, fearful in praises, doing won-*
> *ders?*   Exodus 15:11

Fearful things, unexplainable things happen when we praise God. Paul and Silas were in prison, the door was shut, and they were left in chains. Then, at midnight, these two men put the principle of praise to work:

> *And at midnight Paul and Silas prayed, and sang praises unto God: and the prisoners heard them. And suddenly there was a great earthquake, so that the foundations of the prison were shaken: and immediately all the doors were opened, and every one's bands were loosed.*
>
> *And the keeper of the prison awaking out of his sleep, and seeing the prison doors open, he drew out his sword, and would have killed himself, supposing that the prisoners had been fled. But Paul cried with a loud voice, saying, Do thyself no harm: for we are all here.*
>
> Acts 16:25-28

The prison doors opened and all the chains fell off. Get ready for your miracle. Chains must fall off and other wonders must happen for you in the name of Jesus Christ. If you are tired of where you are, and you desire to move forward, engage this super-natural force and change your story. Stop complaining and start praising God.

If feeding five thousand people was not a miracle, what would you call it? Jesus showed us how He got to that place of miracles:

> *And Jesus said, Make the men sit down. Now there was much grass in the place. So the men sat down, in number about five thousand. And Jesus took the loaves; and when he had given thanks, he distributed to the disciples, and the disciples to them that were set down; and likewise of the fishes as much as they would.* John 6:10-11

Your multiplication starts when you give thanks to God. You are literarily telling Him, "You are all I have, and You are all I need."

3. **Favor with God**: When your efforts are not required for your lifting, that is what is called favor. You will be limited if all you

get is all you labor for. No, that is not what God expects of you. He said:

Be not ye therefore like unto them: for your Father knoweth what things ye have need of, before ye ask him.

Matthew 6:8

The key to favor is praise. After Jesus was raised from the dead and left the earth, His disciples faced many serious challenges. However, Jesus had already taught them what to do when things were not going the way they expected, and now they put that training to work:

Praising God, and having favour with all the people. And the Lord added to the church daily such as should be saved.

Acts 2:47

There was an eruption of favor when the early believers praised God. Kings are known to grant favor unto those they love and admire:

> *And when a convenient day was come,*
> *that Herod on his birthday made a*
> *supper to his lords, high captains, and*
> *chief estates of Galilee; and when the*
> *daughter of the said Herodias came in,*
> *and danced, and pleased Herod and*
> *them that sat with him, the king said*
> *unto the damsel, Ask of me whatsoever*
> *thou wilt, and I will give it thee. And he*
> *sware unto her, Whatsoever thou shalt*
> *ask of me, I will give it thee, unto the*
> *half of my kingdom.*   Mark 6:21-23

The King of Heaven will grant you favor when you have danced before Him in faith. Your praise turns on His unlimited favor. You may not come with any serious credentials, but praise can turn your story around and put you next in line.

Before you start praising God, be sure to remove any blockages:

> *Therefore if thou bring thy gift to the altar,*
> *and there rememberest that thy brother*
> *hath ought against thee; Leave there thy*

gift before the altar, and go thy way; first be reconciled to thy brother, and then come and offer thy gift.   Matthew 5:23-24

Then, release your faith:

But without faith it is impossible to please him: for he that cometh to God must believe that he is, and that he is a rewarder of them that diligently seek him.   Hebrews 11:6

Be expectant:

So shall the knowledge of wisdom be unto thy soul: when thou hast found it, then there shall be a reward, and thy expectation shall not be cut off.
                    Proverbs 24:14

Make the *"sacrifices of joy"*:

And now shall mine head be lifted up above mine enemies round about me: therefore will I offer in his tabernacle

> *sacrifices of joy; I will sing, yea, I will sing praises unto the* LORD.
>
> Psalm 27:6

Remove any doubts. When you are fearful or worried, you are out of order. You are not functioning as God does. He created you for dominion (see Genesis 1:26).

There is no fear in God, no worries at all, so when you think you might die from sickness or disease, that you might fail or be disappointed in life, you are living below His expectations for you. Remember, you are seated with Christ in the heavenly realm (see Ephesians 2:6). God said:

> *A thousand shall fall at thy side, and ten thousand at thy right hand; but it shall not come nigh thee. Only with thine eyes shalt thou behold and see the reward of the wicked.*   Psalm 91:7-8

You can't be given dominion and the ability to subdue the earth and remain a victim. You must have faith in the Word that declares that you were designed to dominate, to operate like God.

You and I were created to operate over and above the rest of creation (see Genesis 1:26). The supernatural that is embedded on the inside of you manifests itself when faith is in operation. Until you believe that the force on the inside of you is important and capable of overcoming any hindrance, you might not see it. Here's what Jesus had to say about it:

> *Jesus said unto him, If thou canst be-lieve, all things are possible to him that believeth.* Mark 9:23

When you operate in the Word of God, you are stepping outside of the natural human ability:

> *Through faith we understand that the worlds were framed by the word of God, so that things which are seen were not made of things which do appear.*
> Hebrews 11:3

Your faith generates raw material for living supernaturally. If you live by your feelings, you will live below expectations.

One of the most important things that calls for our attention is our physical body. We feel hunger, pain, hurts, etc. All too often this is what convinces us that we are mere humans:

*So then they that are in the flesh cannot
please God.* Romans 8:8

Most of the time what our flesh tells us is not true. If you believe the Word of God, at redemption you received a new body by the help of the Holy Spirit. Your body, once corrupt, is now the temple of the Holy Spirit. Therefore, you cannot be defiled:

*If any man defile the temple of God, him
shall God destroy; for the temple of God
is holy, which temple ye are.*
1 Corinthians 3:17

Romans 8:9 tells us that we are no longer *"in the flesh"* now that the Spirit of God dwells in us. Our battle now is setting our affections on Jesus and not on ourselves. You are no longer natural or normal, so don't let the flesh dictate to you any longer. Walk in the Spirit.

God's Word is the Spirit realm that rules the natural world:

> *But he that is spiritual judgeth all things, yet he himself is judged of no man.* 1 Corinthians 2:15

Your faith in the Word brings reward. Your body was intended to work for you, not against you. The Earth was intended to bring you increase, not force you into bankruptcy. Never agree with the dictates of your body and mind when they are acting against the Word of God. The evil of this world was not meant for you. You are of God:

> *Ye are of God, little children, and have overcome them: because greater is he that is in you, than he that is in the world.* 1 John 4:4

> *Herein is our love made perfect, that we may have boldness in the day of judgment: because as he is, so are we in this world.* 1 John 4:17

Jesus said that we could speak to mountains, and they would obey us. That means you are fully in charge here:

> *For verily I say unto you, That whosoever shall say unto this mountain, Be thou removed, and be thou cast into the sea; and shall not doubt in his heart, but shall believe that those things which he saith shall come to pass; he shall have whatsoever he saith.* Mark 11:23

It is very unfortunate that vast majority of believers don't yet know that God did not plan sickness, disease, affliction and premature death for His children. He said:

> *Is there no balm in Gilead; is there no physician there? why then is not the*

health of the daughter of my people re-
covered?   Jeremiah 8:22

God hurts when we are hurting. He has given us an inheritance that makes life worth living, and death and oppression were never part of His plan.

There is a Judgment Day coming:

And the sea gave up the dead which were
in it; and death and hell delivered up the
dead which were in them: and they were
judged every man according to their
works. And death and hell were cast into
the lake of fire. This is the second death.
                    Revelation 20:13-14

Until the time men are finally judged, God has put His Church in charge through the power of the name of Jesus Christ and by the help of the Holy Spirit. We thus become the continuation of Jesus's ministry. Why? Because we are now the Body of Christ.

The will of God is to satisfy you at all times, even with longevity. The evil works of darkness are everywhere, but you have power over them all:

> *Behold, I give unto you power to tread on serpents and scorpions, and over all the power of the enemy: and nothing shall by any means hurt you.* Luke 10:19

Jesus taught in Matthew 13:24-28 about a man who slept, and while he slept, an enemy came and sowed tares in his field. This should never happen to a twenty-first century believer. We are awake, and all tares must be burned to ashes in the name of Jesus.

A major key for provoking the anger of God upon the activities of darkness over our destiny is praise. The Bible says:

> *In every thing give thanks: for this is the will of God in Christ Jesus concerning you.* 1 Thessalonians 5:18

> *For ye have need of patience, that, after ye have done the will of God, ye might receive the promise.* Hebrews 10:36

And who is he that will harm you, if ye be followers of that which is good?

1 Peter 3:13

If we do God's will, we will obtain His promises. It is doing the will of God that guarantees the promises.

In ancient times, the children of Israel found themselves in great distress at the hands of the feared Ammonites. These enemies had convinced other godless nations to join them in harassing and destroying God's people. What should they do? This news greatly troubled King Jehoshaphat, and he did something very wise:

And Jehoshaphat feared, and set himself to seek the LORD, and proclaimed a fast throughout all Judah. And Judah gathered themselves together, to ask help of the LORD: even out of all the cities of Judah they came to seek the LORD.

2 Chronicles 20:3-4

When they had humbled themselves before the Lord in this way, He spoke to them through a prophet that they were not to be afraid. Their victory was assured:

> *Then upon Jahaziel the son of Zechariah, the son of Benaiah, the son of Jeiel, the son of Mattaniah, a Levite of the sons of Asaph, came the Spirit of the LORD in the midst of the congregation; and he said, Hearken ye, all Judah, and ye inhabitants of Jerusalem, and thou king Jehoshaphat, Thus saith the LORD unto you, Be not afraid nor dismayed by reason of this great multitude; for the battle is not yours, but God's. To morrow go ye down against them: behold, they come up by the cliff of Ziz; and ye shall find them at the end of the brook, before the wilderness of Jeruel. Ye shall not need to fight in this battle: set yourselves, stand ye still, and see the salvation of the LORD with you, O Judah and Jerusalem: fear not, nor be dismayed; to morrow go out against them: for the LORD will be with you.*
>
> 2 Chronicles 20:14-17

Not wasting time, they all began praising God:

> *And Jehoshaphat bowed his head with his face to the ground: and all Judah and the inhabitants of Jerusalem fell before the LORD, worshipping the LORD. And the Levites, of the children of the Kohathites, and of the children of the Korhites, stood up to praise the LORD God of Israel with a loud voice on high.*
> 2 Chronicles 20:18-19

They were now ready for battle, and the next morning they set forth. But the way they fought this battle was very unusual. Instead of launching a fight with swords and spears, they went forth singing praises to God:

> *And when he had consulted with the people, he appointed singers unto the LORD, and that should praise the beauty of holiness, as they went out before the army, and to say, Praise the LORD; for his mercy endureth for ever.*   2 Chronicles 20:21

The beautiful thing was that, as God had promised, as they sang praises to Him, He fought their enemies:

> *And when they began to sing and to praise, the LORD set ambushments against the children of Ammon, Moab, and mount Seir, which were come against Judah; and they were smitten. For the children of Ammon and Moab stood up against the inhabitants of mount Seir, utterly to slay and destroy them: and when they had made an end of the inhabitants of Seir, every one helped to destroy another. And when Judah came toward the watch tower in the wilderness, they looked unto the multitude, and, behold, they were dead bodies fallen to the earth, and none escaped.*
>
> 2 Chronicles 20:22-24

Those feared enemies had turned on each other and destroyed each other. All that was left for God's people was to gather up the spoils:

And when Jehoshaphat and his people came to take away the spoil of them, they found among them in abundance both riches with the dead bodies, and precious jewels, which they stripped off for themselves, more than they could carry away: and they were three days in gathering of the spoil, it was so much. And on the fourth day they assembled themselves in the valley of Berachah; for there they blessed the LORD: therefore the name of the same place was called, The valley of Berachah, unto this day.

2 Chronicles 20:25-26

Can you imagine it? It took them three days to gather up the spoils of battle. Then they gathered again for more rejoicing. Friend, whatever the enemy has robbed you of, there is restoration today in Jesus.

When King Saul was troubled by an evil spirit, a search was made for someone who could play anointed music to give him relief. David was the man chosen:

Let our lord now command thy servants, which are before thee, to seek out a man, who is a cunning player on an harp: and it shall come to pass, when the evil spirit from God is upon thee, that he shall play with his hand, and thou shalt be well.

> *And it came to pass, when the evil spirit from God was upon Saul, that David took an harp, and played with his hand: so Saul was refreshed, and was well, and the evil spirit departed from him.*

> 1 Samuel 16:16 and 23

Satan is losing his grip over your destiny even now in Jesus' name. Continue to praise God, setting the atmosphere on fire, and the glory on the inside of you will soon explode. Lift up the Lord, for He is even now setting an ambush against your enemies. Prepare to gather in the spoils of battle:

> *Wherefore David blessed the LORD before all the congregation: and David said, Blessed be thou, LORD God of Israel our father, for ever and ever. Thine, O LORD*

is the greatness, and the power, and the glory, and the victory, and the majesty: for all that is in the heaven and in the earth is thine; thine is the kingdom, O Lord, *and thou art exalted as head above all. Both riches and honour come of thee, and thou reignest over all; and in thine hand is power and might; and in thine hand it is to make great, and to give strength unto all.*

1 Chronicles 29:10-12

Experiencing Supernatural Health

Health is the heritage of the redeemed, Jesus was bruised for our iniquities. The chastisement of our peace was upon Him, and by His stripes we were healed (see Isaiah 53:5). Sickness and disease have been fully taken care of. However, health and healing begins on the inside first, not from outside as many think. The spirit of man will sustain his infirmities:

> *The will to live sustains you when you're sick, but depression crushes courage and leaves you unable to cope.*
>
> Proverbs 18:14, TPT

I want you to see this truth, as described in 3 John 2:

> *Beloved, I wish above all things that thou mayest prosper and be in health, even as thy soul prospereth.*

God works on the inside first. When there is an assurance on the inside, you can conquer any infirmity. We, however, try to work on the outside first, and that is what "messes us up." When you are prospering in your soul, then you will prosper in your body. God's will is that you *"be in health."* The prosperity of your soul will determine how healthy and how wealthy you are:

> *For though we walk in the flesh, we do not war after the flesh: (for the*

weapons of our warfare are not carnal, but mighty through God to the pulling down of strong holds;) casting down imaginations, and every high thing that exalteth itself against the knowledge of God, and bringing into captivity every thought to the obedience of Christ.
2 Corinthians 10:3-5

Your soul controls your body, so if your soul is not developed, your body suffers:

I will praise thee; for I am fearfully and wonderfully made: marvellous are thy works; and that my soul knoweth right well. Psalm 139:14

If your soul doesn't know that health is your covenant right, you will look for health in your flesh or outside of it. Getting enough sleep and enough exercise and eating right are all important, but even these are no substitute for a prosperous soul.

You are a supernatural being, but you can be deceived into walking in the natural. As believers in Christ, we must have *"no confidence in the flesh"*:

> *For we are the circumcision, which worship God in the spirit, and rejoice in Christ Jesus, and have no confidence in the flesh.* Philippians 3:3

There is nothing incurable to the believer. Any impossibility is based on human standards, not God's:

> *For with God nothing shall be impossible.* Luke 1:37

God said:

> *For I will restore health unto thee, and I will heal thee of thy wounds, saith the LORD; because they called thee an Outcast, saying, This is Zion, whom no man seeketh after.* Jeremiah 30:17

No human, however well trained, can bring health to the body. They can only assists the body in doing what it is already programmed to do. This is true of any medication or diet. Health is divine, not natural, and all healing is based on a restored soul.

It's not about you; it's about the power of Jesus' name and God working to bring Him glory. We are even admonished to glorify God in our bodies, which are His:

> *For ye are bought with a price: therefore glorify God in your body, and in your spirit, which are God's.*
> 1 Corinthians 6:20

We give more credit to disease and sickness than we do to the blood of Jesus. We must give Him the right to activate what He has restored for us by faith:

> *All things are delivered unto me of my Father: and no man knoweth the Son, but the Father; neither knoweth any man the Father, save the Son, and he to whomsoever the Son will reveal him. Come unto me, all ye that labour and are heavy laden,*

> *and I will give you rest. Take my yoke upon you, and learn of me; for I am meek and lowly in heart: and ye shall find rest unto your souls.* Matthew 11:27-29

Rest in your soul will bring health in your body. The Scriptures declare:

> *I am crucified with Christ: nevertheless I live; yet not I, but Christ liveth in me: and the life which I now live in the flesh I live by the faith of the Son of God, who loved me, and gave himself for me.*
> Galatians 2:20

> *Bless the LORD, O my soul: and all that is within me, bless his holy name. Bless the LORD, O my soul, and forget not all his benefits: who forgiveth all thine iniquities; who healeth all thy diseases; who redeemeth thy life from destruction; who crowneth thee with lovingkindness and tender mercies; who satisfieth thy mouth with good things; so that thy youth is renewed like the eagle's.* Psalm 103:1-5

Don't leave your territory and become a prey to affliction. The Holy Spirit will get the work done if and when we operate in the Word:

But as it is written, Eye hath not seen, nor ear heard, neither have entered into the heart of man, the things which God hath prepared for them that love him. But God hath revealed them unto us by his Spirit: for the Spirit searcheth all things, yea, the deep things of God. For what man knoweth the things of a man, save the spirit of man which is in him? even so the things of God knoweth no man, but the Spirit of God. Now we have received, not the spirit of the world, but the spirit which is of God; that we might know the things that are freely given to us of God.

1 Corinthians 2:9-12

For the word of God is quick, and powerful, and sharper than any twoedged sword, piercing even to the dividing asunder of soul and spirit, and of the joints and marrow, and is a discerner of the thoughts and intents of the heart. Hebrews 4:12

We don't have a body problem; it's a soul problem. That is why Paul wrote:

And be not conformed to this world: but be ye transformed by the renewing of your mind, that ye may prove what is that good, and acceptable, and perfect, will of God. For I say, through the grace given unto me, to every man that is among you, not to think of himself more highly than he ought to think; but to think soberly, according as God hath dealt to every man the measure of faith. Romans 12:2-3

The psalmist wrote:

I hate them with perfect hatred: I count them mine enemies. Search me, O God, and know my heart: try me, and know my thoughts: and see if there be any wicked way in me, and lead me in the way everlasting.   Psalm 139:22-24

That is why the Word must go into the inner man, to counter every misinformation coming from the outside. You have authority over the body by the power of the Word. This is not positive thinking; it is called a faith declaration. You are calling those things that be not as though they were (see Romans 4:7).

There is a realm you get into in God that is inexplicable to human thinking. That's why it is called the supernatural. It's the realm of miracles. You cannot understand and explain how you move from zero to one thousand overnight.

David was working in the sheepcote one day, and the next day he was ruling the nation. This is a realm designed to make your life an amazement to the world, and this realm can be provoked. Here are some things you can do to make it happen:

1. **Get yourself out of the way**: You must get out of your carnal mind to experience this. Human wisdom cannot operate the supernatural:

> *But the natural man receiveth not the things of the Spirit of God: for they are foolishness unto him: neither can he know them, because they are spiritually discerned.*   1 Corinthians 2:14

This is a realm of trusting God more than your feelings and senses. You have to see things in the Spirit realm. A natural man is limited. He is afraid of a virus because he is not demonstrating the realm of God. Paul declared:

> *And my speech and my preaching was not with enticing words of man's wisdom, but in demonstration of the Spirit and of power.*   1 Corinthians 2:4

It is so exciting that when you don't know what to do, you are in a good place. Count it all joy. You can say, "I don't have it, I can't do it, and it's beyond me. Therefore, I will get out of the way and let God move."

2. **Use the name of Jesus Christ:** When you get hold of that name, you can begin to operate like God, and you are called to operate like Him on the Earth. You are now entering the realm of the impossible:

> *And there appeared unto them cloven tongues like as of fire, and it sat upon each of them. And they were all filled with the Holy Ghost, and began to speak with other tongues, as the Spirit gave them utterance. And there were dwelling at Jerusalem Jews, devout men, out of every nation under heaven. Now when this was noised abroad, the multitude came together, and were confounded, because that every man heard them speak in his own language.* Acts 2:3-6

When the lame man at the Beautiful Gate was healed, Peter spoke up:

Peter saw his opportunity and addressed the crowd. "People of Israel," he said, "what is so surprising about this? And why stare at us as though we had made this man walk by our own power or godliness? For it is the God of Abraham, Isaac, and Jacob — the God of all our ancestors — who has brought glory to his servant Jesus by doing this.

Acts 3:12-13, NLT

When you are using the name of Jesus, nothing is impossible:

And whatsoever ye shall ask in my name, that will I do, that the Father may be glorified in the Son. If ye shall ask any thing in my name, I will do it.

John 14:13-14

By covenant, you have a right to the realm of the Spirit. Why? Because you are in the family. You have the right to know whatever happens in the realm of the Spirit. Jesus said:

He shall glorify me: for he shall receive of mine, and shall shew it unto you.
John 16:14

When you use His name in faith, you can stop the unstoppable by the supernatural:

Wherefore God also hath highly exalted him, and given him a name which is above every name: that at the name of Jesus every knee should bow, of things in heaven, and things in earth, and things under the earth; and that every tongue should confess that Jesus Christ is Lord, to the glory of God the Father.
Philippians 2:9-11

With the power and authority of the name of Jesus, you become lord over every situation. When you use His name, it brings Him back on the scene, as if He were physically here right now.

3. **Be expectant:** Because you have a right to the realm of God by the help of the Holy

Spirit, this gives you great expectations. A believer's expectations do not respect human situations. They go beyond. Once you have imagined something, then begin to activate it, fully expecting it to happen. When you do, it will manifest. It is a lack of respect not to expect God to do wonders. After all, He is *"the God of all flesh"*:

> *Behold, I am the* LORD, *the God of all flesh: is there any thing too hard for me?* Jeremiah 32:27

You cannot be expectant and not shout, not dance, not praise God. Expectation puts your eyes on Jesus Christ alone. The whole world expects this from the Church, and people are confused when they don't see it:

> *For the earnest expectation of the creature waiteth for the manifestation of the sons of God.* Romans 8:19

There must be a love for God, His Word, and His work. He has promised:

He that hath my commandments, and keepeth them, he it is that loveth me: and he that loveth me shall be loved of my Father, and I will love him, and will manifest myself to him.

Judas saith unto him, not Iscariot, Lord, how is it that thou wilt manifest thyself unto us, and not unto the world?

Jesus answered and said unto him, If a man love me, he will keep my words: and my Father will love him, and we will come unto him, and make our abode with him.   John 14:21-23

4. **Walk in revelation:** When praise is on your lips, you flush sickness out of your system:

Bless the LORD, O my soul: and all that is within me, bless his holy name. Bless the LORD, O my soul, and forget not all his benefits: who forgiveth all thine iniq-uities; who healeth all thy diseases; who redeemeth thy life from destruction; who crowneth thee with lovingkindness and tender mercies.   Psalm 103:1-4

Praise ye the LORD. Sing unto the LORD a new song, and his praise in the congregation of saints. Let Israel rejoice in him that made him: let the children of Zion be joyful in their King. Let them praise his name in the dance: let them sing praises unto him with the timbrel and harp. For the LORD taketh pleasure in his people: he will beautify the meek with salvation.

Let the saints be joyful in glory: let them sing aloud upon their beds. Let the high praises of God be in their mouth, and a two-edged sword in their hand; to execute vengeance upon the heathen, and punishments upon the people; to bind their kings with chains, and their nobles with fetters of iron; to execute upon them the judgment written: this honour have all his saints. Praise ye the LORD. Psalm 149:1-7

Why can you do all of this? Because you are now *In Charge!*

OTHER BOOKS BY
DR. ABIOLA IDOWU

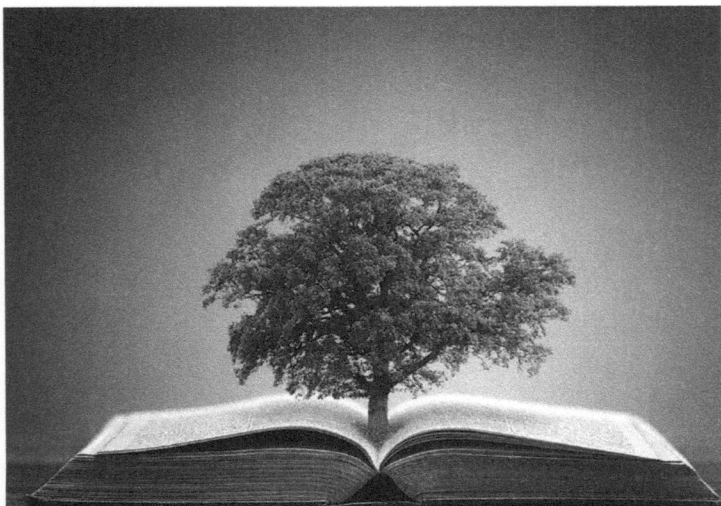

HEAVEN on EARTH

Bishop Dr. Abiola Idowu

WALKING AND LIVING IN YOUR INHERITANCE

BISHOP ABIOLA IDOWU

WEALTH
FAVOUR JOY
GOOD HEALTH
TRANSFORMATION

AUTHOR CONTACT INFORMATION

You may contact the author directly in the following way:

eMail: Bishopidowu@crepa.org

Telephone: (904) 469-5724

www.ingramcontent.com/pod-product-compliance
Lightning Source LLC
Chambersburg PA
CBHW030914090426
42737CB00007B/194